THE **MINI** ROUGH GUIDE TO
GRAN CANARIA

YOUR TAILOR-MADE TRIP
STARTS HERE

Tailor-made trips and unique adventures crafted by local experts

HOW ROUGHGUIDES.COM/TRIPS WORKS

STEP 1

Pick your dream destination, tell us what you want and submit an enquiry.

STEP 2

Fill in a short form to tell your local expert about you dream trip and preferences

STEP 3

Our local expert will craft your tailor-made itinerary. You'll be able to tweak and refine it until you're completely satisfied.

STEP 4

Book online with ease, pac your bags and enjoy the trip! Our local expert will b on hand 24/7 while you're on the road.

PLAN AND BOOK YOUR TRIP AT
ROUGHGUIDES.COM/TRIPS

HOW TO DOWNLOAD
YOUR FREE EBOOK

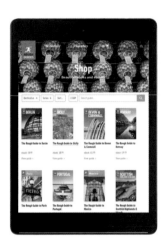

1. Visit **www.roughguides.com/
   free-ebook** or scan the **QR
   code** opposite

2. Enter the code **grancanaria019**

3. Follow the simple step-by-step
   instructions

For troubleshooting contact: mail@roughguides.com

10 THINGS NOT TO MISS

A DAY IN LAS PALMAS

9am

Breakfast. Kick off the day with a leisurely breakfast beneath the trees at a table outside the pretty little Art Nouveau kiosk café in Parque San Telmo.

10am

City vistas. For a panoramic view of the city, take the lift that whizzes you up to the rooftop of the twin-towered Catedral de Santa Ana. When you've taken in the sublime vistas, visit the cathedral itself to enjoy the cool, quiet peace of the delightful cloister.

11am

Casa de Colón. Visit the butter-hued Casa de Colón to admire the ornate latticed balconies and the replica of a cabin from one of Columbus's ships.

Noon

Parque Doramas. Take a bus or taxi to leafy Parque Doramas to admire the splendour of the *Santa Catalina, a Royal Hideaway Hotel,* and visit the Pueblo Canario, a beautifully designed complex of traditional-style island buildings.

1.30pm

Lunch. Hop in another taxi to Parque Santa Catalina. After wandering through the leafy grounds, stop for a light lunch at *Mercado del Puerto* on Calle Albareda. It's a lively gastronomic market with a string of food stalls and tapas haunts tucked beneath nineteenth-century wrought-iron arches – designed by the same architects behind Paris's Eiffel Tower.

DE GRAN CANARIA

3pm

Museo Elder. If you're travelling with children, the Museo Elder is a must-visit. Even if you are not, you will be fascinated by this innovative science and technology museum, set in a building that belonged to the Elder Dempster Shipping Line in the days when Britain had a strong presence on the island.

4.30pm

Playa de las Canteras. Head across the narrow neck of the peninsula to Playa de las Canteras for a swim in the bathwater-warm shallow water, protected by a reef called La Barra. Soak up some sun on the sands, then stroll along the lively promenade until you reach the prestigious Auditorio Alfredo Kraus, home to Gran Canaria's Philharmonic Orchestra.

7pm

Aperitif time. When you are ready to head out for the evening, make your way to Plazoleta de Cairasco where you can check out which exhibitions are on at the cultural centre known as CICCA, then have an aperitif in the elegant square while you watch the sun go down.

8.30pm

Dinner. The square and the surrounding area is an epicurean enclave, peppered with excellent restaurants serving a wide variety of local cuisines. And if you still have energy to burn, head to *La Azotea de Benito* in Plaza Hurtado del Mendoza, a cool rooftop bar where the party continues late into the night.

CONTENTS

ISLAND INSIDER

Whether you are keen to discover Gran Canaria's hidden beaches, historic marvels or culinary experiences, we reveal some of the island's best-kept secrets.

6 LESSER-KNOWN GEMS

Gran Canaria may be best known for its beach-bejewelled coastline but look beyond the sandy swathes to discover natural rock pools or head inland to unearth a different side to the island, from curious painted mountains to a little-known wine route.

1. Risco Caído and the Sacred Mountains of Gran Canaria

A few years ago, nobody had heard of Risco Caído. But since scooping UNESCO recognition in 2019, this pre-Hispanic archeological site is on the radar of in-the-know travellers. Close to Artenara, the island's mountainous interior shelters a smattering of troglodyte dwellings, granaries, cisterns and sacred temples, or *almogarenes*, plus an interpretation centre (www.riscocaido.grancanaria.com) for context.

2. Los Azulejos

The colour-splashed mountains of Los Azulejos – its name a nod to the brightly painted Spanish tiles – are awash with vibrant shades of teal and ochre. A geological marvel caused by oxidization of the mineral-rich rock, this natural phenomenon was revealed over time by erosion. It can be seen on the GC-200 from Mogán to Aldea de San Nicolás, or park by the juice stand and hike the marked trail.

3. Natural rock pools

To the north of the island, the ocean has chewed the volcanic coastline into natural rock pools. As the Atlantic crashes metres away, these mirror-still pools remain calm swimming spots. Some of the best sea pools include Los Charcones; El Altillo; Charco de San Lorenzo; Roque Prieto; Emiliano and El Agujero; Los Roques; and the cascading trio known as Las Salinas.

4. Mirador del Paso de Marinero

For a glimpse of Gran Canaria at its most wild, head to the Mirador del Paso de Marinero in La Aldea. Here, you can

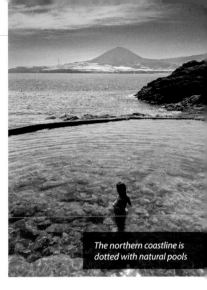

The northern coastline is dotted with natural pools

see a sliver of the untamed west coast, where a knobbly basalt tail snakes around the shore. Visit in the day to see this glorious collision of mountain and sea, or at night to stargaze in clear skies.

5. Gran Canaria Wine Route

Launched in 2021, the Ruta del Vino de Gran Canaria is the Canary Islands' first official wine route. The trail (www.rutadelvinodegran canaria.net) is dotted with over 50 local makers, from wineries and specialist shops to centuries-old *bodegas*, epicurean restaurants, artisanal cheese factories and *bochinches* (food and wine cellars).

6. Arucas

Away from the resort-studded south coast, the north is dotted with traditional towns and villages. The sixteenth-century Arucas is a jumble of pastel-hued buildings wrapping around the Church of San Juan Bautista, whose blue-toned spires pierce the skyline.

THE BEST FOODIE EXPERIENCES IN GRAN CANARIA

Gran Canaria has a rich food scene, from family-run tapas bars and local markets to speciality coffee roasters and generations-old wineries. Fresh seafood, local cheeses, honey rum: island staples are simple and season-driven. However, Canarian food isn't just age-old recipes: a new wave of ahead-of-the-curve chefs is giving a modern twist to classic dishes and collecting Michelin stars along the way.

Bean-to-cup tastings at Finca de la Laja

Cradled in the belly of Valle de Agaete, the 30-acre, family-owned Finca de la Laja (www.bodegalosberrazales.com) grows Arabica beans 1300ft above sea level. Guided tours delve into the island's coffee-making heritage – which took root in the nineteenth century – and offer tastings of a raft of items, including café de Agaete.

Finca de la Laja offers coffee tours and bean-to-cup tastings

Chasing stars

In recent years, a crop of boundary-pushing chefs has put Gran Canaria on the foodie map. In 2023, the island lay claim to four of the Canaries' nine Michelin-starred restaurants, including *Poemas by Hermanos Padrón* (www.restaurantepoemas.com), the brainchild of brothers Juan Carlos and Jonathan Padrón. In Puerto de Mogán, *Los Guayres* (www.losguayres.com) has an epicurean menu masterminded by Alexis Alvarez; *La Aquarela* (www.restaurantelaaquarela. com) champions a sea-to-plate ethos in Patalavaca; and the capital's *Tabaiba* (www.tabaibarestaurante.com) serves experimental dishes.

Market-fresh food

Follow the culinary trail to Mercado del Puerto (www.mercadodel-puerto.net) in Las Palmas de Gran Canaria to discover eateries tucked beneath the arches of a striking Modernist structure – designed by the team behind Paris's Eiffel Tower. Pick from fresh seafood, grilled meats and local specialities like *papas arrugadas* (wrinkly potatoes).

Restaurante Vega

Barranco de Guayadeque is honeycombed with ancient cave dwellings, many now reimagined as subterranean bars, restaurants and homes. It's here you'll find *Vega*, a second-generation haunt that opened in 1981. On an outdoor terrace overlooking the rust-red landscape, diners feast on plates of *conejo frito* (fried rabbit) or *cochinoa la sal*, suckling pig cooked in the style of salted roasted fish.

Quesería La Caldera

At award-winning La Caldera, near Fagajesto, Francisco Javier González Ramos and Tania Rivero Santana breathe new life into a long family tradition of cheesemaking. Sign up for tastings of artisanal cheeses made from the milk of the farm's free-roaming sheep, or learn how to make your own with a masterclass on the terrace.

BEST BEACHES IN GRAN CANARIA

Whether you're after adrenaline-fuelled watersports, an idyllic escape or fun for all the family, there's a beach for everyone.

Best for unspoiled nature: Maspalomas

This UNESCO-protected nature reserve ripples across the southern tip of Gran Canaria, its untamed dunes tumbling down to a 6km-long beach. La Charca lagoon is an excellent birdwatching spot.

Best for people-watching: Meloneras

Maspalomas's stylish little sister, Meloneras unfurls west of the lighthouse for 3km. After dark, the pace shifts up a few gears as beachgoers gather in the trendy bars lining the oceanfront promenade.

Best for children: Amadores

This flour-soft beach is lined by cafés, restaurants and shops. A pair of breakwater piers shelter the bay from the Atlantic waves, while an inflatable children's park and a minigolf course entertain older ones.

Best for active types: Anfi Beach

Fringed by nodding palms, this sweep of icing-sugar sand brings a slice of the Caribbean to Gran Canaria. Intrepid types can try everything from kayaking and paddle boarding to parasailing and flyboarding.

Best for local atmosphere: Puerto de Mogán

Set against a mountainous backdrop, traditional fishing boats bob alongside sleek yachts at Puerto de Mogán. Little Venice is a picturesque tangle of canals and bougainvillea-draped bridges.

Best for escaping the crowds: Güi Güi Chico

Accessed only on foot or by boat, Güi Güi Chico is the larger of a remote pair of coves biting into the west coast. It's a tough

White sands and teal waters at Anfi

two-and-a-half-hour hike from Tasartico unless you persuade a fisherman to take you from Mogán or La Aldea. You arrive first at the dinky 350-metre-long Güi Güi Grande and have to scramble over rocks to reach its bigger sibling Chico, perfect for sunsets.

Best for families with older kids: Puerto Rico

Kayaking, water skiing, paragliding, motorboat rides: Puerto Rico has enough to entertain even the most nonchalant of teens. Marina-side outfits offer dolphin- and whale-watching boat trips and island excursions. Nearby, the Angry Birds Activity Park has its splash zone.

Best for city-breakers: Las Canteras

Las Palmas de Gran Canaria is home to one of the best urban beaches in Europe. Lifeguards watch over kids who splash in the shallows, embark on a game of beach volleyball or join locals in leaping off the hulking rock Peña La Vieja into the sea.

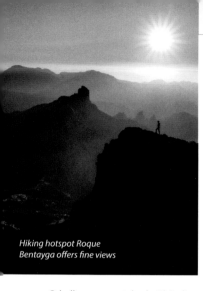

Hiking hotspot Roque Bentayga offers fine views

HIKING ADVENTURES

Gran Canaria is a hiker's paradise, threaded by *barrancos* and littered with archeological sites, with marked trails crisscrossing its UNESCO Biosphere Reserve.

Cruz de Tejeda–Artenara

This 8km hike climbs through fragrant pine forests and offers fine views of Caldera de Tejeda, a volcanic crater blasted wide open by an ancient eruption. The trail passes the Cuevas de Caballero, caves etched with Indigenous rock art, before descending to Artenara. At 1270m, it is the highest village on Gran Canaria and is home to rock-hewn houses and an eighteenth-century cave church.

La Cruz de Tejeda–Teror

This 12km route climbs then dips through cool forest to Teror, a revered pilgrimage site thanks to the Virgin Mary appearing in front of a group of shepherds in 1481. Plaza del Pino is flanked by an eighteenth-century basilica, while fanning streets are lined with colonial Canarian houses punctuated with colourful balconies.

Roque Nublo

One of a pair of landmark rocky pinnacles crowning Caldera de Tejeda, the 80m-tall Roque Nublo, at 1810m, is one of the world's largest free-standing crags. The climb is relatively easy, starting from La Goleta car park, just above Ayacata. The reward at the top:

fine views of Pico de las Nieves – at 1949m, the island's highest peak – and Roque Bentayga, Nublo's smaller sibling (1404m).

Roque Bentayga

This natural rocky fortress has sheltered generations of Indigenous peoples, who built granaries and funerary caves here; walls are etched with inscriptions and paintings. Don't miss the *iralmogarén*, a sacred ceremonial space for the island's earliest inhabitants.

Pico de las Nieves

In the seventeenth century, pits were dug on the mountain to store ice that was later transported five hours on horseback to the ice cream shops in Las Palmas de Gran Canaria. These icy blocks, wrapped in blankets, were also used at the hospital to control epidemics of yellow fever and cholera. At the top of the 1949m-high peak, views stretch south to Maspalomas.

La Fortaleza

La Fortaleza is the site of the last resistance by the Indigenous people against the Castilian conquerors, led by Pedro de Vera, until the 1483 siege that triggered their surrender. It's said that the leaders, Bentejuí and Tazarte, threw themselves off the cliff during that fateful attack. The interpretation centre details the tragic history of the Indigenous people, who probably arrived around 500BC from North Africa and lived peacefully until the Spanish colonized their land.

Tamadaba Natural Park

Part of the UNESCO Biosphere Reserve, the 7500-hectare Tamadaba is the island's largest natural park. Indigenous pine forest shelters woodpeckers, blue chaffinches, kestrels and hawks. Thrusting above the trees, Pico de la Bandera, at 1444m, has its own microclimate, with snowy winters giving way to lush, mist-shrouded summers.

OVERVIEW

The Canary Islands have always been regarded as a bridge between continents. They were the last stopping-off point for Columbus on his journey of discovery in 1492, when emergency repairs were done in Las Palmas de Gran Canaria to one of his three ships. During the sixteenth and seventeenth centuries, the islands were important trading centres through which passed much of the profitable sea traffic between Spain and the Americas. Latin American influences are still visible, in the food and the language, while the architecture reminds us that these were Spanish colonies at a time when the peninsula was at its most wealthy and powerful.

The archipelago lies in the Atlantic Ocean, some 1100km (700 miles) southwest of mainland Spain, and comprises the islands of Gran Canaria, Lanzarote and Fuerteventura to the east, and Tenerife, La Gomera, La Palma and El Hierro to the west. Gran Canaria, the third largest island, is some 195km (120 miles) from the African mainland, on a level with southern Morocco, and covers an area of 1532 sq km (592 sq miles).

A LAND OF EXTREMES

Gran Canaria was formed some 16 million years ago by volcanic activity beneath the Atlantic, at a point where continental drift made the ocean bed particularly unstable. The central mountain massif was once a volcano, and the gorges *(barrancos)* radiating from it were formed by the subsequent process of erosion. Although the island is small, it is extremely diverse. The eastern side is lush and fertile; the north and west bleak and barren; while the expanse of white-sand dunes in the south, barely populated until the 1960s, is now the island's holiday playground. Coastal roads in the west are winding and vertiginous, with stunning views, while away from the coast, all roads lead upwards. The highest point is the Pico de las Nieves – Peak of the Snows – at 1949m (6394ft).

Vegetation on Gran Canaria is as varied as the landscape. The fire-resistant Canary pine *(Pinus canariensis)* rules over the mountainous zone, while a pink rock rose *(Cistus symphytifolius)* clusters around its feet, and varieties of thyme, sage and broom scent the air. The Canary Island spurge *(Euphorbia canariensis)* survives well in the dry southern region, as does tajinaste *(Echium decaisnei)*, a kind of borage, and the Cardon cactus *(Pachycereus pringlei)*, while southern valleys support verdant groves of date palms *(Phoenix canariensis)*. Prickly pear *(Opuntia ficus indica)* is seen all over the northern and central areas; imported from Mexico in the sixteenth century, it was used to cultivate the cochineal beetle. The most unusual flora is the dragon tree *(Dracaena draco)*, which took its name from its red resin known as dragon's blood; this ancient survivor is mostly seen in botanical gardens. The plants you notice immediately – brilliant bougainvillaea, hibiscus and poinsettia, clambering over walls and brightening parks and gardens – are not native but were brought to the islands from subtropical parts and have flourished in the equable climate.

Island birds include the indigenous blue chaffinch *(pinzón)*; greenfinches (not indigenous but very happy here); greater-spotted woodpeckers; the shy Canary chat; and canaries. These are not the bright yellow we are accustomed to seeing, but dun-hued creatures

Hundreds of plant species are endemic to the Canary Islands

Carnival cheer

Carnival began as a religious event, a last celebration before the lean days of Lent, and developed into a riotous affair, with lavish processions and costumed balls. Carnival takes place throughout the Catholic world and the major ones in Gran Canaria and Tenerife are usually staggered so they do not take place at exactly the same time.

that changed colour when they were caged and their breeding controlled.

Gran Canaria has year-round sunshine – some 300 days a year in the south. A strange grey haze called the *panza de burro* – donkey's belly – sometimes shrouds the north. Winter temperatures average 22–24°C (72–75°F), summer sees the mercury hover around 26–28°C (79–82°F), but it often nudges over 30°C (86°F). High season is November to April, but July and August are also popular with Spanish visitors and with English and German families taking advantage of long school holidays.

THE PEOPLE OF GRAN CANARIA

Gran Canaria is part of the Spanish Autonomous Region of the Canary Islands. The population is over 865,000, of whom nearly 380,000 live in the capital, Las Palmas de Gran Canaria. They are, on the whole, relaxed, open-minded people, but keen to stress that they are *canarios*, first and foremost. Islanders refer to mainland Spaniards as *'los peninsulares'*. Spanish *(castellano)* is the language of the islands. However, there are differences from the peninsula, many of which reflect the two-way traffic between the Canaries and Latin America. Final consonants are swallowed, and 'z' is pronounced 's', as in the Americas, rather than the lisped 'th' of mainland Spain. A number of Latino words have been borrowed, too: a bus is a *guagua* and potatoes are *papas*. The strong English influence on the islands has also left some linguistic traces: a cake is a *queque*, and a traditional Canarian knife is a *naife*.

There is a large expatriate population – chiefly English and German – many of whom bought retirement homes or opened bars or restaurants. The official religion is Catholic, though Anglican, Muslim, Mormon and other religions have a presence. Most of the traditional festivals on the island have religious origins. The pre-Lent carnival stands out – a time of elaborate parades, gorgeous costumes and riotous behaviour – but there are other fascinating ones, including the Virgen del Carmen Festival, when the patron saint of the sea is honoured in ports across the island; the Bajada de las Ramas in Puerto de las Nieves; and the mix of religious and secular celebrations for the Virgen del Pino in Teror.

ECONOMY AND ENVIRONMENT

Traditionally, the island's economy has been dependent on agriculture, from sugar cane in the sixteenth century to cochineal, bananas and tomatoes. The principal source of employment today is in the service sector, of which tourism is a major part. EU funds have been used to strengthen infrastructure – roads, airports and hospitals. Works on a new rail line between Las Palmas de Gran Canaria and Playa del Inglés is underway, and the route to the airport is expected to be completed by 2028.

The bounty of the island on display at Mercado de Vegueta

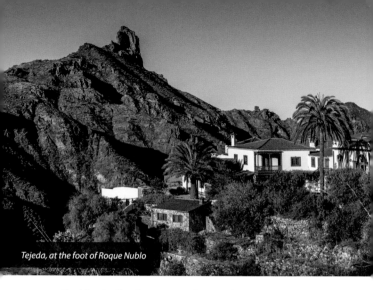
Tejeda, at the foot of Roque Nublo

The island suffers from a water shortage, but locals have long been conscious of their daily water use and implemented water-saving strategies. The issue has been partly overcome by the creation of desalination plants, some fuelled by wind power (and also supplying energy). The drip irrigation system has been widely used on Gran Canaria for decades and several reservoirs across the island play a crucial role in water supply for islanders and the agricultural industry. There is an ongoing surge in solar and wind energy farms across the island, too; part of a wider commitment to renewable energy and sustainability.

THE FUTURE OF TOURISM

A new generation of Gran Canarians that had left the island to travel the world is returning, with an enriched appreciation for their homeland's rich culture, traditions and beauty – and a desire to share this fresh outlook with visitors. Many have reimagined traditional buildings as rural hotels in areas of great natural beauty as part of a thriving *turismo rural* sweeping across the island. This ties in with the trend towards more active holidays on Gran Canaria – from hiking to cycling and coasteering – as well as a surge in digital detoxes, stargazing and foodie experiences. History buffs are flocking to the pre-Hispanic heritage sites and UNESCO World Heritage Sites scattered across the island, while nature fans head to the biosphere reserves swirling around the coastline. A wide range of accommodation is catering to demand, from nature-based boltholes to rural houses and even cave hotels.

REASONS TO VISIT

Although many people visit Gran Canaria for the powdery beaches and warm climate, there is so much more to the island. Las Palmas de Gran Canaria is an enchanting capital city with a vibrant energy. There is a splendid auditorium, a clutch of theatres, numerous good museums, a cultural centre with a varied programme, some excellent restaurants, lively nightlife with open-air bars and rooftop terraces, a thriving marina and an award-winning urban beach.

The central mountainous interior, crowned by the Pico de las Nieves, offers great walking and climbing. Head north to discover the island's rich heritage, from the fascinating archeological park at Gáldar to the iconic church dominating Arucas. This lesser-visited corner of Gran Canaria is the place to go for an authentic slice of island life. You can visit a rum factory; tour a banana plantation and museum, with tastings of jams, wines and other items made from the fruit; and swing by a cheese museum (there's even a festival in Santa María de Guía dedicated to *queso de flor de guía*). The volcanic coastline is sculpted with natural swimming pools, such as El Puertillo and Charco de San Lorenzo, while clear, dark skies beckon stargazers to viewpoints like La Degollada de Las Palomas and Pinos de Gáldar. The *barrancos* are lush with tropical vegetation and riddled with waterfalls. The south is ideal for boating and watersports, with craft and gear to hire; while the vast, empty dunes of Maspalomas feel like a desert by the sea.

HISTORY AND CULTURE

Much of the Canary Islands' history is tied up with that of the Spanish mainland. As a vital point for trade with the Americas, Gran Canaria briefly shared in the prosperity of Spain's Golden Age, although it suffered economic decline thereafter. And in the late twentieth century, the islands, along with Spain, became part of the European Union. But long before the Spaniards ever set foot here, there was a flourishing civilization.

LAND OF THE BRAVE

Tamarán – Land of the Brave – was the proud name given to Gran Canaria by its earliest inhabitants, the pre-Hispanic people of the islands. No one is quite sure of the origins of the Indigenous peoples. Some historians and scientists think they were related to the Canarii people, who lived on the Saharan side of the Atlas Mountains. The few fragments of writing that can be reconstructed are similar to scripts used by the ancient Amazigh (Berber), and some Canarian place names are similar too. But as far as can be deduced, the Amazigh people had no boats, so how they crossed from the African coast remains a mystery.

Nonetheless, archeological evidence has revealed much about the culture of these original islanders. Language and social structure varied from island to island. On Gran Canaria, the rulers were called *guanartemes* and shared some of their power with a *faycan*, who combined the role of judge and priest. Next on the social ladder came the aristocracy, the *guayres*.

The island's earliest inhabitants were a settled, agricultural people, who lived in groups of caves. *Gofio*, toasted flour originally made from barley, was their staple, but they also ate a variety of roots, wild fruits and berries. Pigs, sheep and goats provided meat as well as the materials for shelters, containers and clothes, and milk also came from sheep and goats. Fish formed a part of their diet, even when they had to travel some distance down to the coast to find it.

They did not have the wheel, they knew nothing of metalworking and did not use bows and arrows. Their domestic implements were made from stone and bone or from obsidian, a black, volcanic glass. Porous lava

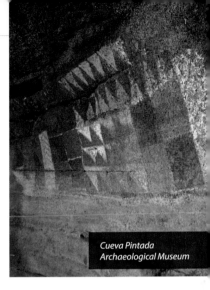

Cueva Pintada
Archaeological Museum

was made into millstones and mortars. Their vessels and containers were made from pottery, wood, leather and woven cane. They mummified their dead and buried them in caves or stone-lined graves, and it is evidence from mummies so far unearthed that has led scientists to place the original islanders' ethnic origins in northwest Africa. The Museo Canario exhibits mummies and skulls in its collection, along with domestic items, remarkably well preserved in the dry climate.

THE CONQUERORS ARRIVE

The first conquering force, in 1403, was led by a Norman lord, Jean de Béthencourt, and funded by the king of Castile, but he failed to take the two main prizes – Gran Canaria and Tenerife. It wasn't until 1478 that another attempt was made, under the aegis of the Catholic Monarchs – Ferdinand and Isabella – of a newly united Spain. As the force was undermanned and the

Indigenous people put up a fight, it took several years to colonize Gran Canaria. Two events contributed to the islanders' downfall: Pedro de Vera arrived as military governor in 1480, and is said to have killed one of the most powerful Indigenous Chiefs, Doramas, with his own hands on the Montaña de Arucas. This coup, along with the capture and conversion two years later of Chief Tenesor Semidan, contributed to the conquest of the Indigenous people, but not before many of them had been killed, starved to death or died by ritual suicide.

De Vera remained governor for 10 years, during which time he had many of the local population deported or enslaved. This, together with an influx of European farmers and entrepreneurs, plus two severe outbreaks of plague, meant that within half a century the Indigenous population was outnumbered. Those

Exhibits on display at the Cueva Pintada Archaeological Museum

who survived had been forcibly converted to Catholicism and many had intermarried with the incomers.

PROSPERITY AND DECLINE

Because of their location, the Canary Islands became a 'successful' example for future Spanish colonization strategies in the Americas. These revolved around slavery and sugar cane, both of which were introduced to

Pirate attack

The Bishop's Palace in Las Palmas de Gran Canaria was one notable victim of Dutch pirate Pieter van der Does' attack; another was the capital's Catedral de Santa Ana. In a display case in the cathedral today there is a splendid bell, a gift from the Asociación Nederlandesa-Canaria in 1999, 500 years after the privateer destroyed the original.

the Americas from the Canaries. The sugar boom on the Canaries only lasted until the mid-sixteenth century, when competition from Brazil and the Caribbean became too strong. While Tenerife was able to switch to a lucrative wine industry, conditions on Gran Canaria were unsuitable for viniculture and the island became something of a poor relation, locked in fierce rivalry with its flourishing sibling. Tenerife came out on top when it became the residence of the Captain-General and location of the first university.

The problems Gran Canaria suffered during the sixteenth and seventeenth centuries were intensified by the fact that the island and her ships were frequently attacked by pirates. The worst outrage was in 1599, when the Dutch buccaneer Pieter van der Does sacked and burned Las Palmas de Gran Canaria.

Gran Canaria began to assert its independence – from Tenerife and mainland Spain – in 1808 when the Napoleonic Wars destroyed Tenerife's wine trade. A junta was formed in Las Palmas de Gran Canaria, calling for 'a patriotic government, independent of the peninsula', but it was unsuccessful. Not until the 1860s did the island's fortunes begin to recover, with the introduction of cochineal, the red dye produced from a beetle of the same name that feeds on cacti. The boom was short-lived, as the invention of cheaply produced aniline dyes brought a virtual end to the industry. Poverty and unemployment forced many islanders to emigrate to the Americas, mainly Cuba and Venezuela.

It was only in the 1880s that things really began to get better, largely due to Fernando León y Castillo, a local politician who became foreign minister in the Spanish government. With the collaboration of his brother, Juan, an engineer, he embarked on a project to transform Las Palmas de Gran Canaria into the major port on the island. Within about six years, the Puerto de

Casa de Colón, or Columbus' House

la Luz was dealing with most of the steamship trade that passed through the islands.

WAR AND RECOVERY

The last of the briefly successful monocultures was bananas, introduced by the British in the late nineteenth century. But World War I had a disastrous effect on the trade, creating more poverty and more emigration. After Cuba won freedom from Spain in 1898, there were calls for Canarian independence, but most people simply wanted the division of the archipelago into two separate provinces. Formalization of this came in 1927 but no new economic solutions had been found when the three-year Spanish Civil War began in 1936, initiated by Francisco Franco, military governor of the Canary Islands. He spent the last night before launching his coup in the *Hotel Madrid* in Las Palmas de Gran Canaria.

After the civil war and World War II, the Canaries, like the rest of Spain, suffered from isolation and economic hardship. Things improved a little in the 1950s, when Spain was once more recognized by the international community, but it was the advent of tourism in the following decade that really turned the tide. Franco remained in power until his death in 1975, when his authoritarian regime was replaced by a democratic government. The new Spanish Constitution of 1978 created the Autonomous Region of the Canary Islands – now one of seventeen such regions. The archipelago is not completely separate from Spain but the island government, the Cabildo Insular, does have a great deal of freedom.

The islands have enjoyed considerable commercial freedom and tax exemptions ever since the nineteenth century, but when Spain became a full member of the European Union, fiscal changes had to be introduced. To protect trade and industry, the Puerto de la Luz and the industrial area round Arinaga were confirmed as a Free Trade Zone, governed by a local consortium.

The economy is not unhealthy, but it does need some support. The agricultural sector finds it difficult to compete in the wider market. Until the end of 1995, Spain guaranteed a market for Gran Canaria's bananas but since then, despite EU subsidies, the

BRITISH INTERESTS

There is a street in Las Palmas de Gran Canaria called Alfredo Jones, another called Tomás Miller, and the science museum is the Museo Elder. They were named after three of the British businessmen who had the most influence on Las Palmas de Gran Canaria in the nineteenth and early twentieth centuries. There was a fourth – James Swanton – who seems to have been overlooked when street names were doled out. British influence on the island was far-reaching. Swanton and his young cousin, Thomas Miller, ran an import–export business, started in the 1820s. It flourished at the height of the cochineal boom. When aniline dyes killed demand, Miller began importing coal from Cardiff. The Santa Catalina jetty in the new port was financed by a second generation of Millers and Swantons; major shipping lines with offices in the port were British-owned – one was the Elder–Dempster Line, in whose premises the Museo Elder is housed; and the water, electricity and telephone services were all set up by Englishmen. Sir Alfred Jones never lived on the island, but he founded the Grand Canary Coaling Company and financed the construction of the *Hotel Santa Catalina*. These wealthy businessmen established *Club Inglés* (*British Club*; still in Calle León y Castillo) and founded the first golf club. They built houses in the leafy Ciudad Jardín (Garden City) in Las Palmas de Gran Canaria and on the hills outside, in Tafira and Santa Brígida, still regarded as desirable places to live. For several decades at least, Gran Canaria was an informal colony of the British Empire.

Mass tourism changed the face of Gran Canaria

industry has plummeted. Production costs are high, and bananas need a lot of water – a scarce commodity. The island is a major supplier of tomatoes for the European market, but countries with lower labour costs, such as Morocco, have been able to undercut the Canarian growers. The only real money-spinner is tourism.

TOURISM AND THE ENVIRONMENT

The creation of the resorts of San Agustín, Playa del Inglés and Maspalomas in the 1960s, catering to sun-seeking northern Europeans, changed the face of Gran Canaria. This, together with the opening of Gando international airport in 1974, made tourism the main industry. The economy skyrocketed and islanders gained employment for most of the year.

In the past few decades, Gran Canaria tourism has been repositioning and reinventing the destination, shining a light on sustainable travel, from hiking and biking holidays to foodie experiences

Water is a scarce resource that must be handled carefully

and archeological tours. This new model aims to complement the classic sun and beach holidays for which Gran Canaria first gained its popularity and to ensure the tourism industry has a positive impact on the island – now, and in the future.

For ecological and economic reasons, the Cabildo Insular has made huge efforts to diversify the tourist industry and protect the environment. Many areas have been designated natural parks and nature reserves; in fact, over 66,000 hectares (154,000 acres), some 40 percent of the island, is protected to some degree. Active environmental protection groups exert a steadying influence.

WIND, WATER AND FIRE

Water on the island is not only in short supply but, until relatively recently, was also in the hands of private suppliers. This has always been a contentious issue and, in the south, it has been taken out of private hands and is run by a franchise called Canaragua. Water shortages have been alleviated to some extent by desalination plants – there are two huge ones run by a private company, Acciona Agua. Wind power has been introduced to keep costs down, and the gigantic wind farm at Pozo Izquierdo on the gusty east coast is the foremost example of this.

In July 2007, the island suffered from its worst forest fires in over fifty years. Low humidity, high temperatures and strong winds contributed to the devastation that led to the evacuation of over 5000 people from their homes. Around 20,000 hectares (50,000 acres) of ground was burnt, particularly in the mountainous region around Mogán. Fortunately, no lives were lost. Two years later, another wildfire in the south of the island damaged some 25,000 hectares (62,000 acres) and forced a mass evacuation, but the region recovered remarkably well.

A GENTLER IMAGE

Gran Canaria's tourist industry suffered less than that of the rest of Spain during the economic downturn of the early twenty-first century, and visitor numbers have risen dramatically in recent years. The industry has been given a new direction, with less emphasis on sun, sea and sand, and more on environmentally conscious aspects of the island. EU funds have helped in the promotion of the turismo rural initiative – helping to convert traditional buildings into country hotels. The opening up of the *caminos reales* (royal paths) in Gran Canaria's interior is part of a drive to attract walkers and cyclists. It has certainly paid off: the island's dramatic volcanic landscape has lured international athletes to its world-class cycling and trail running events.

In 2018, UNESCO classified Gran Canaria's biosphere reserve a Starlight Destination thanks to its proximity to the equator, high altitudes and low levels of light pollution. The island has a network of astronomy viewpoints: standouts can be found in Las Cañaditas, La Degollada de las Yeguas, Paso del Marinero, La Sabinilla and La Cruz del Siglo.

Oenophiles should follow the Gran Canaria Winery Route – the only certified wine route in the Canary Islands. The trail is peppered with *fincas*, wineries and *bochinches* where local rural makers continue to work and live as they have for years. Visits help to preserve this traditional way of life.

There has also been a resurgence of interest in the island's pre-Hispanic past and cultural heritage. A highlight is the UNESCO-protected Risco Caído, a pre-Hispanic *almogarene* (temple) in the Sacred Mountains of Gran Canaria, a biodiverse landscape contoured by cliffs, sheer ravines and twisted lava formations. In Gáldar, one of the two ancient capitals, which calls itself the Ciudad de los Guanartemes (City of Rulers), most of the streets have Indigenous names, and the state-of-the-art Cueva Pintada Archaeological Museum traces the island's long history. An increasing number of children are being given Indigenous names, such as Tamara or Tenesor, and a favoured name for bars and restaurants is Tagoror, which means a place of assembly. Perhaps this is all part of a move to establish a new sense of island identity, while remaining very much a part of Europe.

Gran Canaria boasts the only certified wine route in the Canary Islands

IMPORTANT DATES

***c.* 1st–2nd centuries BC** First human settlements in Canary Islands.

AD1477–83 Spanish force lands on the island and subdues Indigenous peoples.

1492 Columbus briefly stops at Las Palmas de Gran Canaria before sailing to America.

***c.* 1500** Sugar cane introduced and enslaved Africans imported. From 1554, the sugar industry declines.

1700–1950 Poverty forces widespread emigration to Latin America.

1830 A short economic boom follows the introduction of the cochineal beetle.

1852 Isabella II declares the Canary Islands a Free Trade Zone.

1890 The British introduce bananas as a monoculture.

1911 Self-administration council – Cabildo Insular – introduced.

1927 The Canary Islands are divided into two provinces. Las Palmas de Gran Canaria becomes capital of the eastern province.

1936 Franco, military governor of the Canary Islands, initiates the three-year Spanish Civil War.

1956 The first charter plane lands on Gran Canaria. Tourism rapidly develops into the most important industry.

1974 Gando international airport opens.

1978–82 New Spanish Constitution joins the two island provinces to form the Autonomous Region of the Canary Islands.

1986 Spain joins the EU and negotiates a special status for the Canaries.

1995 Islands integrated into the EU but retain important tax privileges.

2002 The euro becomes the national currency.

2005 Islands hit by Tropical Storm Delta, causing severe damage.

2007 Summer fires devastate the Mogán region.

2009 More fires in Mogán cause damage but the area quickly recovers.

2010–11 Gran Canaria (and Tenerife) buck the trend by attracting greater numbers of tourists despite the economic downturn.

2014 A record number of foreign tourists (3.13 million) visits Gran Canaria. Several oil spills affect beaches in the southern part of the island.

2020 Covid-19 pandemic hits Gran Canaria, obliterating travel.

2022 Tourism on the islands starts to recover as Covid-19 restrictions are lifted.

The spectacular dunes at Maspalomas

OUT AND ABOUT

Gran Canaria is not a huge island but what it lacks in size, it makes up for in diversity. You only have to travel the short distance south from capital city Las Palmas de Gran Canaria to the dry dunes of Maspalomas, then explore the lush Barranco de Agaete in the northwest, scale the mountainous central heights, or spend a peaceful day in one of the coastal fishing ports, and you will feel that you have visited a small continent.

LAS PALMAS DE GRAN CANARIA

Las Palmas de Gran Canaria ❶, the sprawling capital of Gran Canaria, has a population of over 400,000 people, nearly 80 percent of whom make their living in the service industries. The city is divided into distinct enclaves. To the south is the UNESCO-listed historical core, Vegueta, which is separated by a busy dual carriageway from Triana, an attractive old shopping district peppered with cafés and Art Nouveau buildings. The traffic-filled Avenida Marítima and noisy Calle León y Castillo lead to the next points of interest: Parque Doramas and the Muelle Deportivo yacht harbour. A further busy stretch, either following the sea or on a parallel road inland, marches to the huge Puerto de la Luz and Parque Santa Catalina. From here, a grid of streets links the city and the beach, Playa de las Canteras, the island's original holiday playground before resorts sprang up along the south coast.

Between these points are the busy commercial streets around Avenida Mesa y López and Ciudad Jardín, where flowers blossom in walled gardens and flags fly above government buildings. At the far northern tip is La Isleta, a working-class district with a clutch of excellent fish restaurants; up on the hills behind is the Ciudad Alta where many of the capital's citizens live and work.

The pastel-hued facades of Triana

TRIANA

Whether you come straight from the airport or on a bus trip from the south, you are likely to arrive at **Parque San Telmo** , for this is the site of one of the city's two bus terminals and the place where taxis wait to whisk passengers to other parts of town. There's a children's playground in the square and a pretty little chapel, the Ermita de San Telmo, its unassuming whitewashed facade concealing ornate and gilded interiors. Opposite, an Art Nouveau kiosk, decorated with gleaming tiles, serves drinks to patrons at tables beneath towering *fisco* trees; and the Quiosco de la Música bandstand stages regular concerts. At the back of the square, a plaque on a military building informs that here, on 18 July 1936, Franco announced the coup that initiated the Spanish Civil War.

To the left of the square, the pedestrianized **Calle Mayor de Triana** is flanked by a string of attractive facades – some colonial in style, others Art Nouveau – fronting a medley of shops, from a tiny fabric store and old-fashioned tobacconists to well-known high street brands. To the right, the narrow, pretty streets are reminiscent of the Triana district in Seville from which this area took its name, and are lined by smart boutiques and antiques shops, tucked between tapas restaurants and bar terraces. The Librería del Cabildo Insular (www.libreriadelcabildo.com) on the corner of Cano and Travieso, is stocked with a wide choice of books and maps on the islands.

Calle Cano is also the place to find the **Casa-Museo Pérez Galdós** Ⓑ (www.casamuseoperezgaldos.com; Tues–Sun 10am–6pm; guided tours on the hour). The building where Spanish novelist Benito Pérez Galdós was born in 1843 (see box) is a splendid example of Canarian architecture, built around a courtyard and decorated with portraits and furniture from his houses in Madrid and Santander, many of which he designed and made himself. Further south on Calle Alfonso XIII is the beautiful blue building of the **Casa Africa**, (exhibitions Mon–Fri 10am–6.30pm; www.casafrica.es), which promotes African culture and celebrates relations between Europe, Africa and South America.

Close by is a little jewel of a square, the **Plazoleta de Cairasco**. The *Hotel Madrid*, one of the oldest in the city, serves meals and drinks at outdoor tables beneath the palms till late at night. At the north end, the splendid **Gabinete Literario**, floodlit after dark, is an Art Nouveau treasure and designated a 'Monumento Histórico

---

FAMOUS SON

Benito Pérez Galdós (1843–1920) is widely regarded as one of the greatest Spanish novelists and playwrights, and many believe he would have received the Nobel Prize for Literature had it not been for his unpopular political views. His books and plays offer an inside view of Spanish life, and he was unusual in that he did not restrict himself to the world of just one social class. Born in Las Palmas de Gran Canaria, he spent much of his life in Madrid and Santander, where he became increasingly involved with politics. A staunch republican, he was elected as a senator for Madrid in 1910, and for Las Palmas de Gran Canaria when he returned in 1914. His greatest play, *Electra*, received its premier in the theatre named after him in Triana (www.teatroperezgaldos.es).

Artistico'. Once a theatre, it is now home to a literary society (www. gabineteliterario.com), and also houses a restaurant-café with comfortable chairs on a shady terrace.

To the side of the little plaza runs the **Alameda de Colón**, at the north end of which, near a bust of Columbus, is the white-washed, colonial-style **Iglesia de San Francisco**. Destroyed in the fire of 1599, following Dutch pirate Pieter van de Does' attack, it was rebuilt during the seventeenth century, then became a paro-chial church after the monks were ejected (as they were through-out Spain in 1821). At the south end of the *alameda* (tree-lined avenue), in an imposing building with stone-framed doorways, is a cultural centre, known by the acronym **CICCA**, where La Caja de las Canarias, a munificent savings bank, funds exhibitions, films, music and theatrical performances.

You are close now to the major highway (Calle Juan de Quesada) that separates Triana from Vegueta, but before you cross there's another attractive square to swing by. It is officially called Hurtado de Mendoza, after an early twentieth-century painter, but usually known as **Las Ranas**, or The Frogs, because the long pool that runs down the centre is fed by two spouting amphibians. A cluster of bars and street food spots can be found around Frogs Square and Monopol Boulevard, and the area is always buzzing with a young crowd at night. Nearby is an imposing library building, also fre-quented by students from the university a short distance up the highway; there is some student accommodation in Triana.

VEGUETA

The historic centre of Las Palmas de Gran Canaria has a character all of its own. This was once the aristocratic quarter, and its cobbled streets are lined with colonial buildings punctuated by intricately carved balconies and opening onto palm-filled interior courtyards, glimpsed when their huge, polished doors are ajar.

Twin-towered Catedral de Santa Ana

At its heart, in **Plaza de Santa Ana** , is the twin-towered **Catedral de Santa Ana** (Mon–Sat 10am–4.30pm; www.catedral-santaana.com; access only through Diocesan Museum). Started in 1497, it wasn't completed until the twentieth century and is a glorious mishmash of architectural styles – Gothic, Renaissance and Neoclassical. Intricate details on the facade and many of the statues inside are the work of the Canary Island sculptor, José Luján Pérez (1756–1815).

The adjoining **Museo Diocesano de Arte Sacro** (hours as above; entrance in Calle Espíritu Santo) has a lovely cloister, the Patio de los Naranjos (Orange Trees). Among the sacred paintings and artefacts on display is an impressive modern series, *Stations of the Cross*, by local artist Jesús Arencibia. If you don't want to visit the museum and cathedral, you could take the modern lift (same hours; separate charge), which will whisk you to the top of one of the towers for a great view over the city.

Among the magnificent buildings in the plaza, the **Palacio Regental** may be the star. It is largely seventeenth century, although the facade dates from 1867. The Canarian balcony is older, as is the huge and splendid doorway, above which is the coat of arms of the kingdoms of León and Castile. Little remains of the adjoining **Palacio Episcopal** (Bishop's Palace) except an ornate single-storey facade. It was a victim of the fire of 1599, when Dutch privateer Pieter van der Does destroyed most of the town (see page 27).

Huge bronze dogs, the island's heraldic animal, guard the cathedral, and at the other end of the palm-lined square is the elegant nineteenth-century building housing the **Casas Consistoriales** (Offices of Island Government).

Beyond the square is the little Plaza Espíritu Santo with its unusual domed fountain in the centre. From here, Calle Dr Chil leads to the Museo Canario. This is a street of splendid houses with carved wooden balconies and intriguing, shady courtyards, most of which are now the homes and offices of lawyers.

The Vegueta food market on Calle Medizábel (Mon–Sat 6.30am–2pm) sells fruit and vegetables as well as fresh fish, local cured meats and cheeses. There are good local tascas and bars dotted throughout the surrounding streets.

THREE VEGUETA MUSEUMS

The first of three Vegueta museums that deserve attention is the **Museo Canario** Ⓓ (www.elmuseocanario.com; Mon–Fri 10am–8pm, Sat–Sun 10am–2pm) on Calle Dr Verneau. It houses the Canary Islands' largest collection of pre-Hispanic objects – pottery, tools, mummies and skeletons, and dozens of skulls, lined up in glass cases like macabre ornaments. Here, you will see the ochre-coloured figure of the Idolo de Tara, a fertility goddess, copies of which are on sale in souvenir shops all over the island. There are also scale models of Indigenous dwellings and a replica of the Cueva Pintada in Gáldar (see page 73). Further east, at Ramón y Cajal 1, in a beautifully refurbished eighteenth-century former hospital, is the San Martín Centro de la Cultura Contemporánea (www.sanmartincontemporaneo.com; Tues–Sat 10am–9pm, Sun 10am–2pm), a contemporary art gallery and concert hall.

The **Casa de Colón** Ⓔ (www.casadecolon.com; Mon–Sat 10am–6pm, Sat 10am–3pm) is an endearing little museum, with ornate doorways and beautiful latticed balconies. Colón is the Spanish name for Columbus, and it is claimed, with no supporting evidence, that he stayed here while one of his ships was being repaired. The thirteen exhibition rooms and three large patios feature a replica of the cabin of *La Niña*, one of Columbus's fleet, nautical maps and charts, and a collection of pre-Columbian artefacts from Ecuador

The Casa de Colón is one of the city's most splendid buildings

Columbus's prayer

A plaque on the wall of San Antonio Abad, the tiny chapel next to the Casa de Colón, claims that the explorer stopped to pray on this spot before setting off on his voyage of discovery.

and Mexico. The house was the birthplace, in 1927, of the operatic tenor Alfredo Kraus.

The **Centro Atlántico de Arte Moderno** (CAAM; www.caam.net; Tues–Sat 10am–9pm, Sun 10am–2pm) is worth visiting mainly because it is a wonderful exhibition space – white walls, marble stairs and acres of glass, concealed behind a traditional facade. It has a good reputation as an educational and cultural centre, but visitors may find its changing exhibitions are generally of less interest than the building itself.

PARQUE DORAMAS AND THE PUEBLO CANARIO

Leave the old town now and hop on a bus (from Teatro Pérez Galdós on the Triana side of the highway, or from Parque San Telmo) to **Parque Doramas**, in a prosperous, leafy part of town known as the Ciudad Jardín. Amid tropical greenery in front of the ultra-smart **Santa Catalina, a Royal Hideaway Hotel by Barceló**, a large statue dedicated to the vanquished Chief Doramas shows Indigenous people leaping from a rocky fountain.

To the left of the hotel is the **Pueblo Canario 🄵**, a little complex of traditional island buildings with café tables in a central plaza. This Canarian village was designed in the 1930s by brothers Néstor and Miguel Fernández de la Torre, to try to spike the interest of early tourists in island ways. Costumed folk dancing displays are held in the central square here every Sunday (11am–noon; free). The **Museo Néstor** (closed for restoration until further notice), dedicated to the better known of the brothers, is part of the complex. Born in Las Palmas de Gran Canaria, Néstor (1887–1938), always known simply by his first name, spent much of his life in Paris, Madrid and Barcelona, where he became famous for his sensuous paintings and imaginative stage designs. He returned to the island in later life with a heightened awareness of his roots and painted two series of works, *Atlantic Poem* and *Visiones de Gran Canaria* – both can be seen in the museum. There are also rooms dedicated to Canarian music and architecture.

Opposite the park is the Club Natación Metropol swimming and sports club (www.cnmetropole.com). Beside it, an underpass leads below the Avenida Marítima to the **Muelle Deportivo** Ⓖ, the yacht harbour, from where transatlantic yachtsmen set out, and visitors can take catamaran trips. The waterfront promenade is lined with restaurants, cafés and shops, protected from the traffic on the road above. Adjoining the harbour area are Varadero Maritime Club (www.club-maritimovaradero.com) and Real Club Náutico (www.rcngc.com) beside the Playa de Alcaravaneras, a stretch of beach frequented by families, so busiest at weekends.

PARQUE SANTA CATALINA

If you want to do any shopping, head inland along broad Calle Mesa y López, where most of the big stores are found, including a branch of Spain's largest department store, *El Corte Inglés*. Otherwise, it's not far

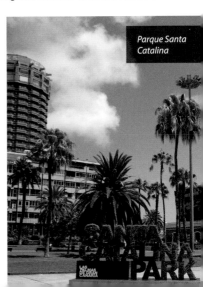

Parque Santa Catalina

to the next point of interest, **Parque Santa Catalina** Ⓗ. Although dotted with palm trees and vivid flowerbeds, this, like San Telmo, is more of a square than a park, but much bigger and busier. There is always a sense of activity, with visitors and local people chatting at outdoor cafés. Here, you can get local information from a small kiosk, board one of the open-topped hop-on-hop-off *guagua turística* buses for a spot of sightseeing, or book tickets in the Fred Olsen office for the ferry to Tenerife. The company runs a free bus to Agaete to connect with the ferries.

AROUND THE PORT

On the port side of the park is the striking **Museo Elder** (www. museoelder.org; Tues–Thurs 9.30am–7.30pm, Fri–Sun 10am–8pm), a wonderful science and technology museum housed in a building that belonged to the Elder-Dempster Shipping Line, but has extended upwards and outwards. There are lots of interactive exhibits to amuse children, as well as an industrial robot spot-welding a car, a model of Foucault's pendulum, an incubator where patient visitors can watch chicks hatching from eggs, and an IMAX cinema.

A landscaped pedestrian area leads from the museum to the **Muelle Santa Catalina** Ⓘ, in front of which an enormous, sail-like awning conceals a subterranean bus terminal. To the left, a shiny commercial centre, **El Muelle** (www.ccelmuelle.es), overlooks the port. Further north is the Poema del Mar (www.poema-del-mar.com; daily 9.30am–5.30pm), a modern aquarium that's breathed new life into this part of town.

PLAYA DE LAS CANTERAS

The stretch north from here along the huge **Puerto de la Luz** is all industrial buildings and traffic-clogged roads, so cross back to Parque Santa Catalina and make your way, via Calle Luís Morote, through the maze of streets to the beach. Do not miss gastronomic hub **Mercado del Puerto** (www.mercadodelpuerto.net), only a few metres away, a perfect spot to linger over a plate of tapas washed down with an ice-cold beer at any time of the day.

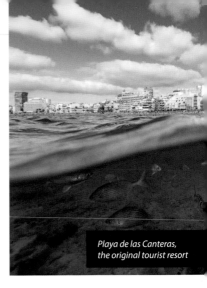

Playa de las Canteras, the original tourist resort

Playa de las Canteras ❶ is the 3km (2-mile) stretch of sand that made the city Gran Canaria's very first tourist resort. It is lined with hotels and restaurants, some of which have been here since the 1960s heyday. A wide ocean-front promenade runs the length of the beach and beyond; this busy walkway is dotted with tall palms, sun umbrellas that restaurants set out by the sea, and a few bright market stalls piled with carvings and jewellery.

Las Canteras is gaining popularity again within tourists, who prefer the city vibe to that of the southern resorts, and a wave of young remote workers hang out in this area. The top end of the beach has nets for volleyball and beach tennis, and the sea is often speckled with surfers. The natural reef, **La Barra**, a few hundred metres out, turns this stretch of coast into a natural lagoon, safe for children and non-swimmers.

LA ISLETA AND AROUND

At the northern tip of the beach, where the peninsula is at its narrowest, old wooden fishing boats are pulled up on the sand. Follow

The Museo Elder keeps visitors entertained for hours

the road behind La Puntilla, a wind-tousled point jutting out to sea, to reach the old fishermen's quarter of **La Isleta ⓚ**.

Here, you can visit the sombre Castillo de la Luz, now used as an exhibition centre (Tues–Sat 10am–7pm, Sun until 2pm) and the location of the **Fundación de Arte y Pensamiento Martín Chirino** (www.fundacionmartinchirino.org), which showcases the sculptures of local artist Martín Chirino.

The main reason to come to this corner of the island is to scale the highest peak at **Las Coloradas** for a sweeping view of the foam-tipped sea, the mountains and the city. It's a long, steep climb, though, and you would do better to take a taxi or a bus from Parque Santa Catalina.

At the southern end of Playa de las Canteras, beyond the reef's protective arm, constant onshore winds create ideal conditions for surfers. This area has been smartened up, with a landscaped promenade leading to the **Auditorio Alfredo Kraus**, home to the Philharmonic

Orchestra of Gran Canaria. A mammoth bronze statue of the tenor, who was born in the city, stands proudly outside. Seen from a distance, the sand-coloured building appears to rise from the sea, and in some lights blends into the hills behind. Across the road stands the huge **Las Arenas** commercial centre, which adjoins the stark Palacio de Congresos conference centre. From here, the arched bridge on the motorway heading northwest looks close enough to touch.

THE EAST

The lushest and loveliest corner of Gran Canaria is the eastern region. It takes in the verdant Barranco de Guayadeque, where a small community of people live in caves, as well as a string of towns with well-preserved historic centres. It nudges into the area south of Arinaga, where strong winds power Pozo Izquierdo, Gran Canaria's biggest wind farm. Those same winds help competitors during the world championship windsurfing competitions held at Pozo Izquierdo. There are also surfing schools and other watersports available to tourists. Driving down the GC-1 motorway from the airport or from Las Palmas de Gran Canaria, you will not be aware of the treasures that lie only a few kilometres inland. Faceless as most motorways, it is lined with factories,

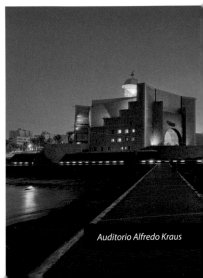

Auditorio Alfredo Kraus

Discover local flora at Jardín Canario

out-of-town megastores and an airforce base, all set in a bare, scrubby landscape. It is, of course, the fastest way to reach the areas of interest, but if you are not in a hurry, you could explore via minor roads.

JARDÍN CANARIO

If you take the Santa Brígida road (GC-110) to the south-west of Las Palmas de Gran Canaria, you can visit **Jardín Canario Viera y Clavijo** ❷ (www.jardincanario.org; Mon–Fri 7.30am–6pm, Sat–Sun 10am–6pm; free), Spain's largest botanical garden and abundant in endemic plants from the Macaronesia region – the Canaries, Azores and Madeira islands. If you just want to make an excursion from Las Palmas de Gran Canaria to the garden, there are several buses from San Telmo and Plaza Santa Catalina. The botanical garden lies close to the suburb of Tafira Alta, with elegant, early twentieth-century villas and beautiful gardens. The Jardín Canario is delightful, established in 1952 by the Swedish botanist Eric R. Sventenius and laid out along the steeply sloping side of a gorge.

A new main entrance and car park allows visitors to reach a flatter section where a cactus garden features an amazing selection of specimens from all over the world, many introduced to the island from the Americas in the seventeenth century. Just past the wooden bridge, there is a string of ponds with cascades and specimens of *Laurisilva* (bay laurel), which covered much of the island before the Spanish conquest but have long since been destroyed.

There is also an avenue of dragon trees *(Dracaena draco),* which were once believed to have healing properties, and a grove of *Pinus canariensis,* the indigenous pine tree. Allow a good couple of hours to visit the garden, because it is quite extensive and there is so much to see. Those with mobility problems might want to avoid the steep, cobbled paths to the ridgetop, though the rest of the garden is flat and smooth.

CALDERA DE BANDAMA

Just past Tafira Alta and Monte Lentiscal (the two prosperous suburbs virtually run into each other), drivers can take a left turn to the **Caldera de Bandama**. The volcanic crater is 1km (0.5 mile) wide and 200m (655ft) deep, and the best view of it is from the volcanic peak next door, the Pico de Bandama (574m/1,883ft), which has an observation platform and small bar – and you can drive to it. From here, you also take in magnificent views of the entire north and east coasts of the island. On a clear day, you can sometimes see the neighbouring island of Fuerteventura to the northeast, while to the west looms the central massif.

Adventurous visitors can climb down into the crater itself, via a steep path that is visible from the rim – it takes about thirty minutes. At the bottom is an abandoned farmhouse, shaded by two enormous eucalyptus trees, and the outlines of terraced fields where vines were once cultivated. South of the caldera, which is the Spanish word for cauldron but has become the international geological term for a volcanic crater, lies one of the best golf courses on the island – and the oldest in Spain – the Real Club de Golf de Las Palmas, with its classical MacKenzie design. The club was founded at the end of the nineteenth century by some of the English expatriates who were so influential in the growth and prosperity of the city, and who were eager to indulge in one of their favourite forms of recreation.

TELDE

Back on the main road, turn left at San José on the GC-80 to **Telde**
❸. Follow signs to San Juan or the Centro Histórico and park as soon
as you can, because Telde, the second-largest town on the island, is
bedevilled by narrow, one-way streets and far too much traffic. There
is a large modern section that is of little interest to visitors, but the
old town, a protected conservation area since 1981, is well worth a
stop. It centres on the attractive Plaza de San Juan, shaded by mature
trees and surrounded by colonial-style houses with beautiful mosaic
tiles and intricately carved balconies. Lording it over the square is the
Iglesia de San Juan Bautista (daily from 10.30am but only if a custo-
dian is available). Building began in 1519, but the neo-Gothic towers
are early twentieth-century additions. It houses a beautiful sixteenth-
century Flemish altarpiece showing six scenes from the life of the

Virgin, acquired when the town grew rich from the sugar trade. It is because the altarpiece is so valuable that the church is usually only open during services or when a guardian is available. The church's other treasure is an image of Christ made in Mexico from corn cobs. Just off the square is a children's park, with brightly coloured birds in an aviary. The street that links San Juan with the other historic district, San Fernando, is named, like many others in Gran Canaria, after Fernando and Juan León y Castillo, the brothers who transformed the port of Las Palmas de Gran Canaria. They were born in Telde and their home is now the **Casa-Museo León y Castillo** (www.fernandoleonycastillo.com; Tues–Sun 10am–6pm). It contains Spanish paintings from the sixteenth to the twentieth centuries, along with sculpture and porcelain as well as a library.

CUATRO PUERTAS

Telde was one of the two capitals before the Spanish arrived (Gáldar was the other) and the Indigenous people have left us an interesting archeological site, just off the GC-100 from Telde to Ingenio. **Cuatro Puertas** (always open; free), also known as Montaña Bermeja after the colour of its dark reddish stone, consists of a main chamber with four huge entrances. A shallow, semicircular enclave in the rock is thought to have been a sacrificial site, and the open space in front of the chamber was a tagoror, a place of assembly. The main cave is easily accessible, with excellent information boards explaining what you are looking at.

INGENIO

Around 5km (3 miles) along the GC-100 lies **Ingenio ❹**, an attractive little town famous for its delicacies such as *pan de puño* (fist bread), sold all over the island, and *sopa de la Virgen* (Virgin's soup). It was a prosperous sugar-refining centre in the sixteenth century (a model sugar press stands at the eastern approach to the town), but agriculture – chiefly tomato-growing – is the mainstay these days. Narrow alleys of whitewashed houses lead to the tiled **Plaza de la Candelaria**, where modern fountains contrast with a white, colonial-style church and the ochre-coloured town hall. Beside the church, bronze statues of women washing clothes add interest to another fountain. Between the church and town hall is the Tourist Office, which gives access to the Interpretation Centre of the Historical Heritage of Ingenio (tel: 928 783 799; call for opening times). This interactive space provides an illustrated journey back in time from the current history of the municipality to the pre-Hispanic era of the island.

BARRANCO DE GUAYADEQUE

Just before you reach the next town, Agüimes, 2km (1 mile) away, you will see a sign to the **Centro de Interpretación Arqueológica** (Tues–Sun 9am–5pm). This is the best route to take to the **Barranco de Guayadeque ❺**, well surfaced and less tortuous than the one from Ingenio, which also leads to the Interpretation Centre. The *barranco* is one of the most beautiful valleys on the island. Its steep slopes are honeycombed with cave dwellings (see box, page 57), and lush flora still thrives – cacti, tajinaste, palms and poppies, among other plantlife. The *barranco* is also home to one of the biggest lizards in the world – the *Lagarto canarión;* sparrow hawks can be seen in the skies and the sound of woodpeckers reverberates in the pine woods. There are still several functioning wells in the gorge; the Morro Verano, at 170m/555ft, is the deepest.

The *barranco* is for serious walkers, and there is a reliable organization in Agüimes that arranges hikes if you want to go with a group (see page 96). If you visit alone, make sure you have warm clothes for the chilly heights, strong shoes and plenty of water. However, there is much that can be enjoyed without doing anything too strenuous. The surfaced road continues for 9km (5 miles) or so beyond the Interpretation Centre, passing glorious scenery and reaching two cave villages, both still viable communities, with tiny chapels, a bar and rudimentary restaurant, and houses bright with geraniums. The road ends at the best-known cave restaurant, the *Tagoror*.

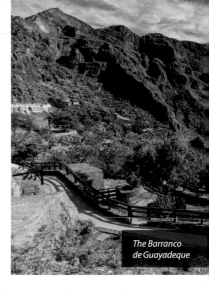

The Barranco de Guayadeque

AGÜIMES

Agüimes ❻ is one of the most appealing towns on the island. It's a place where the Ayuntamiento (Town Hall) takes seriously the job of preserving and improving the environment, and fostering conservation-conscious tourism – and it shows. The outskirts of the town, where there is a bus station and a public swimming pool, is pleasant enough, but the **Casco Histórico** is the place to go.

Spotless, narrow streets of ochre- and terracotta-coloured houses – several of them converted into *casa rural* accommodation – lead to the shady main square, **Plaza de Nuestra Señora del Rosario**, flanked by bars and cafés. Here, and in other parts of town, a smattering of bronze statues has been erected, portraying rural life and local characters. The Neoclassical **Iglesia de San Sebastián** (daylight hours) at one end of the square, is a designated Monumento Histórico Artístico and has works by island sculptor José Luján Pérez. The Museo de Historia de Agüimes (Tues–Sun 9am–2pm & 3–6pm) at Calle Juan Alvarado y Saz 42 is also worth a visit if you're interested in local history. The tourist office, on Plaza San Antón, has an

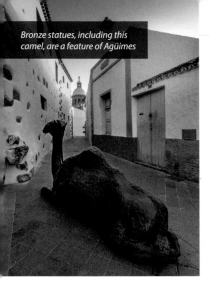

information centre with old photos and historical pieces. Soft classical music spills out from hidden speakers around a bronze statue of a female cellist.

ARINAGA

For a real contrast, make the short trip from Agüimes to sleepy little **Arinaga**. As you will soon realize, this is a windy stretch of coast, but one much in favour with windsurfers. There is also a marine reserve and diving centre, at **Playa del Cabrón**. What is most immediately obvious, south of Arinaga, are the huge, graceful and surprisingly quiet wind turbines producing energy at the Pozo Izquierdo plant. Pozo Izquierdo beach is the site of events in the PWA World Cup Championships.

THE SOUTHERN RESORTS

The southern resorts of Gran Canaria are having a renaissance. A wave of new modern resorts, like Meloneras and Amadores, is emerging alongside the traditional mainstays, such as San Agustín and Playa del Inglés. Huge investments in infrastructure have made this corner of the island even more accessible and sustainable than ever. What all Gran Canaria's resorts have in common is year-round good weather, miles of rolling sands flanked by ocean-front promenades, watersports facilities, hotels and apartments with lush gardens and landscaped swimming pools; and restaurants, bars and shops by the score.

SAN AGUSTÍN AND PLAYA DEL INGLÉS

Whether you are coming direct from the airport, from Las Palmas de Gran Canaria, or from Agüimes, you will approach the resorts on the GC-1 motorway. The first one, **San Agustín ❼**, was also the first to be built, in 1962. There is a fairly small, safe beach and a clutch of attractive hotels and apartments, most set in lush gardens of palms and poinsettia, some with their own swimming pools. The

CAVE DWELLERS

The Centro de Interpretación is a helpful introduction to the life of the valley and its people, and displays some of the items – pottery, bones and textiles – that have been recovered from caves. More items are on display in the Museo Canario in Las Palmas de Gran Canaria. The *barranco* was the most densely populated gorge on the island during pre-Hispanic times. Early inhabitants farmed the slopes and even went down to the coast to fish, as the remains of sea-snail and limpet shells indicate. Numerous grain stores have been excavated and many mummified bodies were found in caves when interest in the area was stimulated at the end of the nineteenth century. The cave villages that exist today are rapidly being depleted. In 1970, there were some 450 inhabitants, now there are only about ninety. There are two chapels, and a functioning school, although it has fewer than a dozen pupils. Some crops are still grown – potatoes and corn in the higher regions, almonds on the lower slopes and on the valley floor – and some goats, pigs and sheep are kept, but most people now work in bars and restaurants, catering to the tourists.

Paseo Costa Canaria

signature five-star Meliá property reopened in 2023 as the ultra-sleek *Paradisus Gran Canaria*, an all-inclusive resort right by the beach and one of the latest additions to the island's luxury hotel portfolio. You can walk along the promenade from San Agustín to **Playa del Inglés** ❽, a well-known resort with an array of hotels and apartments to suit all budgets and tastes. Huge investment has been pumped into the resort, helping to maintain its popularity as a holiday destination over the decades. The recently revamped **Yumbo Centre** attracts a large crowd when the sun goes down, with the bars and clubs catering to the LGBTQ+ community. For a drink with a view, head up to the flying saucer-shaped *Atelier Cocktail Bar*, which sits on the rooftop above the *Bohemia Suites*.

The beach is the main event, of course. The **Paseo Costa Canaria** is an attractive pedestrian promenade, lined with villa complexes and bright with tropical blooms. The walkway runs the length of the sandy swathe, from Playa de las Burras all the way to the Maspalomas dunes. Descend via stairs or escalators to the **Paseo Marítimo**. Protected by awnings from the heat of the sun, this is a 2km (1.25-mile) stretch of bars, restaurants and shops.

MASPALOMAS AND MELONERAS

Maspalomas ❾ is divided from Playa del Inglés by a spectacular stretch of **dunes**, sprawling across an area of 4 sq km (1.5 sq miles), which in 1994 was designated a nature reserve in order to preserve the ecosystem. Walk through *Hotel RIU Palace Maspalomas* to the Mirador de las Dunas, the best viewpoint for taking in the epic scale of the dunes. Please note, you can't walk freely over the dunes now, but there is a well-marked path to cross them. Even if you protect your feet from the hot sand, it is still hard-going and takes over an hour.

If you follow the beach around the headland instead, it takes half the time, and you will pass a popular nudist stretch en route as well as *Chiringuito 7*, where a proudly flying rainbow flag nods to its thriving LGBTQ+ community. Brushing up to the dunes, the Maspalomas golf course is the first-ever pay and play club in Spain. The surrounding enclave of villas and bungalows known as

THE COUNT'S VISION

The Conde del Castillo de la Vega Grande de Guadelupe, an aristocrat with a pedigree as long as his name, had a family home in Telde, in a building that is now the town hall. He also had large tracts of unused and seemingly useless land in the barren south of the island. Nobody lived there, nothing would grow there and the land was a liability. In the early 1960s, however, as the tourist boom swept through mainland Spain, the count came up with a scheme that would change the face and the economy of Gran Canaria. Out of the desert, he constructed what are now the resorts of San Agustín, Playa del Inglés and Maspalomas. Tour companies, quick to spot a potential gold mine, soon moved building contractors in. Where else would you find streets named after tour operators as you do in Maspalomas? Within two decades, the south of Gran Canaria had mushroomed into a huge holiday complex, attracting visitors from northern Europe, mainly on all-inclusive package holidays, providing employment for islanders and further enriching the man who masterminded the project.

The dunes of Maspalomas offer a wonderful sense of freedom

Campo Internacional forms another barrier between the two neighbourhoods.

The main road swoops past the turn-off inland towards **Aqualand water-park** (daily 10am–6pm; www.aqualand.es) and **Palmitos Park** (same hours; www.palmitospark.es; joint tickets available), with exotic birds, plants and aquarium. You will also pass **Holiday World Maspalomas Centre** (daily 5pm–noon; www.holi-dayworldmaspalomas.com) before continuing to El Faro, the lighthouse that marks the south-ernmost point of Gran Canaria. Here, a thousand-year-old palm grove and **La Charca**, a mirror-still lagoon attracting migratory and breeding birds, form part of the Maspalomas Dunes Nature Reserve. This natural beauty provides a magnificent backdrop for some of the best hotels on the island, such as the superb boutique *Seaside Grand Hotel Residencia*, a member of the Leading Hotels of the World.

To the west of the lighthouse, Maspalomas merges with the newly developed **Meloneras** ❿, a small town that's grown into Gran Canaria's main tourist resort. A 3km-long oceanfront prom-enade is lined by ultra-modern luxury hotels, stylish bars, restau-rants and high-end shops. There's a casino and coast-hugging golf course, plus a conference centre that moonlights as a cultural hub for live music, plays and sporting events. The resort is flat and accessible, so it's a good option for people with reduced mobility.

PASITO BLANCO, SALOBRE AND ARGUINEGUÍN

The GC-1 motorway continues towards Puerto Mogán, passing through a series of tunnels, some over 2km long. The first community west of Meloneras (on the old coast road) is **Pasito Blanco**, a smart marina and private residential resort mainly of interest to sailing enthusiasts. On the right-hand side of the GC-1, a diversion leads towards the luxe *Salobre Hotel Resort and Serenity*, the only resort in the Canary Islands with two golf courses. Next comes **Arguineguín**, a working fishing port with a lovely community feel, and **Anfi**, a sun-soaked resort with flour-white beaches and a marina flanked by restaurants, bars and shops. A buzzy beach club, *Maroa*, has an oceanfront bar, sunloungers and daybeds. Nearby, *Radisson Blu Gran Canaria Mogán* offers a slice of luxury to discerning types.

PUERTO RICO AND AMADORES

A trailblazing tourist development of the 1970s, **Puerto Rico** ⑪ unfurls from the lip of a sheer ravine, its apartments built into the cliffs. At the foot of the rocky flank is a cluster of bars, restaurants and tropical gardens, and a golden-hued beach wrapping around a sheltered bay. The shopping and entertainment hub of Mogán Mall is breathing new life into the resort, while children will love the **Angry Birds Activity Park** (www.activityparkcanarias.com; Thurs–Mon 10am–6pm).

Puerto Rico has a serious reputation as a sailing centre, and members of its club have won several Olympic medals. Naturally, **Puerto Deportivo** caters for visiting fishing and watersports enthusiasts. There are diving centres and sailing schools, deep-sea fishing trips, dolphin-spotting trips in glass-bottomed catamarans, and simple pleasure trips that wend along the scenic coastline.

To the west of Puerto Rico, **Amadores** is a modern resort with an inviting beach kissed by turquoise waters. The two resorts are connected by a 3km-long oceanfront promenade, above which a scattering of cliffside hotels offers fine sea views (many with lifts whisking guests straight down to the beach below). *Amadores Beach Club* is a chic haunt with a champagne bar and luxe daybeds, while *ANFI Tauro Golf Club and Resort* beckons golfers to its Atlantic-facing fairways along the coast.

La Charca

La Charca, part of the Maspalomas nature reserve, is a little lagoon to which migratory and breeding birds, frightened away by human activity, are being encouraged to return. Moorhens, herons and kestrels have ventured back to its reed beds and ospreys have occasionally been seen.

TAURITO AND PUERTO DE MOGÁN

Just before you reach Puerto Mogán, you will see on your left Taurito, a self-contained family-friendly resort with watersports, a large lido, a waterpark and a handful of hotels and apartments. Built around a complex of seawater canals with delicately arched bridges, **Puerto de Mogán** **⑫**, known as Little Venice, is almost impossibly pretty. The windows and flat roofs of its two-storey apartments are

Postcard-pretty Mogán

outlined in shades of blue, green and ochre, the walls smothered with multicoloured bougainvillaea and trailing geraniums.

There are two ports here: the working one that was once the town's *raison d'être* and from which a fishing fleet still operates, and the **Puerto Deportivo**, where luxurious yachts bob in the water. This leisure port is lined with cafés and restaurants, all offering wonderful views and boat-fresh fish and seafood. The buildings that line the streets behind the harbour are equally picturesque; most are holiday apartments belonging to the *LIVVO Hotel Puerto de Mogán* (see page 146). Luxury accommodation abounds, from *Cordial Mogán Playa*, built in a traditional Canarian style with lush botanical courtyards and home to one of the island's five Michelin-starred restaurants, and the five-star *Radisson Blu Resort and Spa*, the latest to turn heads on the hotel scene.

Submarine Adventure offers trips in a yellow submarine, and glass-bottomed boats ply back and forth between here, Puerto

Rico, Anfi and Arguineguín. However, most visitors are content simply to wander the streets and sit in the pavement cafés, or make for the small, sheltered beach to the east of the marina.

On Friday, a huge market spills along the quay, selling African carvings, bead jewellery, aromatherapy oils, island cheeses, fresh fruits, and beach sarongs. Busloads of tourists arrive from neighbouring resorts around 10.30am and are whisked away with their purchases in the afternoon.

MOGÁN

The road inland wends its way up the fertile, fruit-producing *barranco* to Mogán. In season, you may be able to buy ripe papaya, mangoes and avocados from streetside stalls. Just before the town, a windmill stands sentinel by the road in the tiny hamlet of El Molino de Viento – which means windmill. Surrounded by jagged mountains, **Mogán** ⑬ is a sleepy little place with a picture-postcard church dedicated to San Antonio; colourful gardens in the central plaza; and towering palms outside the town hall.

GOING WEST

The west of Gran Canaria is for those who like a challenge. It is the area least visited by tourists; the roads are vertiginous and villages few and far between. But there are stunning rock formations and mountain landscapes, marvellous views and a chance to experience a region that feels quite remote, although it's only a few hours' drive from Las Palmas de Gran Canaria.

THE MOUNTAIN ROUTE

The road from Mogán (GC-200) twists and turns on its way to San Nicolás de Tolentino, cutting through rocks of red, grey and gold and passing isolated houses where convolvulus clings to crumbling walls. To your right soar the Montaña de Sándara, the Montaña de las Monjas, and the peak of Inagua, all nudging over 1400m (4600ft) high. To the left, three deep gorges run down to the sea. The first is the **Barranco de Veneguera**, where a track – which should only be attempted in a 4WD vehicle – leads 10km (6 miles) through banana plantations to a lovely, unspoiled beach. The barranco is part of the

The beach at Güi-Güi

Parque Rural del Nublo and cannot be developed for tourism.

The road running through the next gorge, the **Barranco de Tasarte**, is in better condition, and also culminates in a pretty beach. From the third gully, the **Barranco de Tasártico**, there is a long, arduous hike through the **Reserva Natural Especial de Güi-Güi**, where 3000 hectares (7400 acres) of land are protected to safeguard the vegetation clinging to the rocks. Those who go the distance will be rewarded with an idyllic little beach. Just past the Tasarte turning, to the right of the road, is **La Fuente de los Azulejos**, where oxidization has turned the rocks bright green. Opposite, a roadside bar sells papaya juice and aloe vera.

SAN NICOLÁS DE TOLENTINO

As the road begins to straighten, you come to the village of **Tocodomán**. Here, you will find **Cactualdea** (www.cactualdea.es; daily 10.30am–5pm). This 'cactus village' is home to more members of the spiky plant family than you knew existed, all well labelled and set among palms and dragon trees. There is also a replica Indigenous cave, a restaurant serving typical Canarian dishes, wine-tasting opportunities and, of course, a gift shop.

You won't be able to miss the fact that swathes of land here are covered in plastic. Beneath the sheets grow tomatoes, the crop that is the mainstay of the region and of its only proper town, **San Nicolás de Tolentino** (officially known as La Aldea de San Nicolás). The town does not have a lot going for it, but it's a friendly place that tries hard to attract visitors. A tourist office on the right as you enter town offers informative leaflets and has *artesanía* items for sale, the woven textiles showing distinct Latin American influences. The town used to be a craft centre but these days weaving and pottery are hobbies rather than industries. There

Los Azulejos

are a few small hotels and a couple of restaurants offering 'home-style cooking'.

PUERTO DE LA ALDEA

Some 3km (2 miles) down the road is **Puerto de la Aldea** ⑭ – which simply means 'port of the village'. The harbour is tiny, but there seems to be enough fish brought in to keep a few restaurants flourishing. Beside a pebbly beach is a smartly tiled promenade; parallel to it runs a shady garden with stone picnic tables set beneath pine trees. At the far end lies **El Charco** (The Lagoon), a fairly nondescript pond for most of the year but on 11 September the site of the Fiesta del Charco, when local people attempt to catch fish with their bare hands and to duck each other in the water. The origins of this curious custom are uncertain, but it is believed to date from pre-Hispanic times. *Lucha canaria* (wrestling) matches and *juego del palo* (stick-fighting) competitions are an integral part of the festival.

An Indigenous settlement close by, **Los Caserones**, has yielded a great many archeological finds, including the bones of a Verdino dog, the emblem of the Canary Islands. The remains of the settlement can be seen on a small hill.

THE COASTAL ROAD

The journey along the coast demands concentration. The road wends between bare rock on one side and steep cliffs, plunging straight into the ocean, on the other. Fortunately, two *miradores*

Fishing fiestas

The Fiestas del Carmen, celebrating the patron saint of fishermen, take place throughout July in Arguineguín and Puerto de Mogán. Celebrations include firework displays, concerts and dances and culminate in a maritime procession, led by a decorated boat carrying the statue of the Virgin.

(viewpoints) have been created at points of particular beauty, so drivers can safely stop to admire the views. The first is the **Mirador del Balcón**, the second the **Andén Verde**. To the north, the craggy coastline runs up to the Punto de Góngora; straight ahead, across miles of dark blue sea, lies Tenerife, crowned with the peak of El Teide, at 3718m (11,898ft) the highest mountain in Spain. The road here is prone to rock falls and is occasionally inaccessible. The first phase of a new motorway between El Risco and Andén Verde, which darts through a 3km tunnel, provides an alternative route.

PUERTO DE LAS NIEVES

There are still many curves to navigate before you arrive at **Puerto de las Nieves ⑮** (The Harbour of the Snows). The name derives not from any freak snowfall but from Nuestra Señora de las Nieves, the Madonna of the Snows, patron saint of the local fishermen. Her tiny chapel, known as the **Ermita de las Nieves** (by appointment only outside Mass times), houses a real treasure, a sixteenth-century Flemish triptych attributed to Joos van Cleve, depicting the Virgin and Child flanked by saints Francis and Anthony. The decorated wooden ceiling above the choir is said to be Mudéjar, the architecture of the Moors who remained in Spain after the reconquest in the late eleventh century.

In the harbour, fishing boats bob gently beside a jetty, where wooden decking has been laid down for the benefit of sunbathers who can't find a comfortable spot on the pebble beach. There is a sheltered bay, which is good for swimming. A cluster of restaurants lines the quay, serving excellent fish at reasonable prices. They get very busy at weekends, when people from Las Palmas de Gran Canaria come for lunch. Otherwise, the main bursts of activity are the arrivals and departures of the ferries to Santa Cruz de Tenerife, run by the Fred Olsen line (a free bus from Las Palmas de Gran Canaria connects with the port).

*The view from
Andén Verde*

A great deal of investment has gone into the village in an attempt to compensate for the declining fishing industry. *Occidental Roca Negra Hotel* has been built close to the remains of an Indigenous cemetery, though the development on the whole has been sympathetic. A promenade called the Paseo de los Poetas has been constructed, and some low-rise apartment blocks and villas have sprung up in the streets behind it, blending well with the single-storey fishermen's cottages. At the southern end of the village, at the foot of the dramatic coastline, the stump of the **Dedo de Dios** (Finger of God) rises from the sea. The 'finger' itself, once a famous local landmark, was destroyed by a storm in 2005.

AGAETE

Return to the main road and almost immediately you are in **Agaete** ⑯, where a number of the houses have carved wooden balconies. In the Plaza de la Constitución, as you enter the town, stands the

Agaete hooks around a pretty bay

imposing, nineteenth-century Iglesia de la Concepción, and nearby, off Calle Huertas, the **Huerto de las Flores** (Tues–Sat 10am–4pm; free) is a small botanical garden planted with some rare trees. On the outskirts is the **Parque Arqueológico de Maipés** (www.arqueologiacanaria.com; Tues–Sun 10am–5pm in winter, until 6pm in summer), an Indigenous necropolis.

The town stands at the head of the **Barranco de Agaete**, a fertile, emerald-green gorge signposted **El Valle** (The Valley). It's a lovely place to drive or walk. Avocados, oranges, lemons and mangoes grow on terraces, clinging to the steep valley walls. Tall Canary palms, solitary agaves and prickly pears gradually give way, on the upper slopes, to the Canary pine.

The road only tracks as far as Los Berrazales. Just before you reach the little village, a dirt track diverts to the atmospheric *Finca Las Longueras* (www.laslongueras.com), a *hotel rural* housed in a nineteenth-century colonial mansion (see page 148). Another place worth dropping by is **Bodega Los Berrazales** (www.bodegalosberrazales.com; daily 10am–5pm), a winery, coffee plantation, fruit orchard and cheesemaker in the 200-year-old *Finca de la Laja*, at the foot of the Tamadaba cliffs. Sign up for a farm tour and tasting to sample the bounty of the land. Nearby, the excellent *Restaurante Romantica* is run by the same family and serves a menu of farm-to-fork cuisine; it also sells a curated collection of local handicrafts and has a Canarian kitchen-garden planted with herbs, fruits and vegetables that's open to customers.

THE NORTH

There are some 700 hectares (1730 acres) of protected land in the north of the island; the best known is the **Reserva Natural de los Tilos de Moya**. Away from these reserves, the terrain is fairly barren, for the forests of bay laurel (*Laurus canariensis*) that once coloured the landscape green were cut down in the sixteenth century to provide fuel for the sugar industry. Yet more land was cleared to make way for bananas, introduced as a monocrop by the English more than three centuries later.

The principal crop today is still bananas, many of which are grown in mammoth plastic tunnels. In marked contrast to the sparsely populated west coast, this small area encompasses half a dozen towns: Gáldar, Guía, Moya, Arucas, Firgas and Teror. All are worth visiting and all involve circuitous, winding roads. It is often easier to return to the main coastal road between towns, rather than take what looks like the shortest route.

GÁLDAR

The hill on which **Gáldar** ⑰ is set resembles an extinct volcano, with the town clustered at its feet. It is only about 8km (5 miles) between Agaete and Gáldar, but the pace of life seems to shift up a few gears. Park as soon as

You say tomato

The tomato industry is not as prosperous as it once was, as it now faces stiff competition from Moroccan growers. Despite this, the region still exports some 100,000kg (220,000lbs) of early varieties a year. The *tomate aliñado* is a popular tapas dish: a huge local tomato comes sliced and dressed in olive oil, vinegar and lashings of garlic.

you find a space because traffic can often be heavy, and the one-way streets are confusing. Gáldar is known as the Ciudad de los Guanartemes (City of Rulers), as it was the seat of Tenesor Semidan, one of the island's two Indigenous Chiefs. The town is proud of its heritage and many of the streets and squares have Indigenous names. Post-conquest Gáldar was founded in 1484 and was the capital of Gran Canaria before Las Palmas de Gran Canaria.

The **Iglesia de Santiago de los Caballeros**, in a shady square, was built on the spot where Semidan's palace supposedly stood. Begun in 1778, it was the first Neoclassical building on the island. It houses a number of statues attributed to José Luján Pérez (1756–1815), who was born nearby in Santa María de Guía. The Ayuntamiento (Town Hall), in the same square, has a huge dragon tree in its courtyard. Planted in 1718, it is said to be the oldest in

Iglesia de Santiago
de los Caballeros

the archipelago. At the side of the square, you will find the tourist office and the Teatro Municipal.

The Patrimonio Histórico – the department in charge of cultural affairs – was somewhat slow to exploit Galdár's legacy, but the **Museo y Parque Arqueológico Cueva Pintada** (www.cuevapintada.com; Tues–Sat 10am–6pm, Sun 11am–6pm) is now open on Calle Audiencia, in the town centre, on the site of the Painted Cave. Visitors can buy tickets in advance on site and through the website. Another important archeological site, reached by a lane running through banana plantations towards the coast, is the **Poblado y Necrópolis de la Guancha**, consisting of the remains of circular tombs and a number of houses where ancient mummies were found.

SARDINA

From the roundabout to the west of Gáldar (the same way you came in), the main road west leads to **Sardina**, a tiny resort hugging a small beach, popular with snorkellers and protected by dark, volcanic rocks. A harbourside restaurant offers excellent fish dishes and a view of the beach. Sardina is quiet during the week but attracts people from Gáldar and Las Palmas de Gran Canaria at weekends. North of the village, a lighthouse stands on the windy Punta de Sardina.

SANTA MARÍA DE GUÍA

The next town, travelling east from Gáldar at the same roundabout, is little **Santa María de Guía** ⑱, usually just known as Guía, famous for its award-winning *queso de flor*. This is a cheese made from sheep and cow milk, mixed with the juice of cardoon thistle flowers for added flavour. A traditional cheese festival is held here at the end of April and beginning of May and continues in nearby Montaña Alta.

There are some attractive, brightly painted houses in Guía's Casco Histórico, and an imposing, two-towered church in the Plaza

Grande (not as huge as its name might suggest) where a market is held every Tuesday morning.

CENOBIO DE VALERÓN

Take the main road now for Moya, but turn off first where you see signs to the **Cenobio de Valerón** ⑲ (www.arqueologiacanaria.com; Tues–Sun winter 10am–5pm, summer 10am–6pm). *Cenobio* means convent and this complex of some 300 caves, hollowed out of the soft, volcanic rock, was once believed to have been a place where *harimagüadas* – young virgins – were detained in order to protect their purity until they married. However, it is now widely accepted that the caves were grain stores, which were easily defensible because of their isolated position.

MOYA

The GC-75 – the next turning off the main road – winds uphill to friendly, sleepy little **Moya** ⑳. There is a helpful tourist office and an impressive church, **Nuestra Señora de Candelaria**, begun in

BRINGING DOWN THE BRANCHES

Puerto de las Nieves and Agaete are renowned for a festival known as Bajada de las Ramas (Bringing Down the Branches), celebrated with great enthusiasm on 4–5 August each year. Residents of the two communities gather branches from the hillsides and carry them down to the harbour, where they whip the waves with them before laying them at the feet of the Virgin of the Snows. Although this provides a religious context, the ritual has pagan origins, and, like many festivals, was intended to bring both rain and fertility. It's a high-spirited occasion, with lots of music and dancing, feasting and frolicking, and people come from all over the island to take part.

Cenobio de Valerón

the sixteenth century but with many later additions. It is home to some interesting pieces of sculpture, including a fifteenth-century cedarwood figure of the Virgin of Candelaria, and several works by Luján Pérez, but unfortunately it is often closed except for early evening services.

Moya is the birthplace of the island's best-loved poet, Tomás Morales (1885–1921) and his former home, the **Casa-Museo Morales** (www.tomasmorales.com; Tues–Sun 10am–6pm) stands in the square opposite the church. It's an intimate little place featuring first editions of Morales' work, his Remington typewriter and an abundance of photos, paintings, poems and other personal artefacts. Look out for the bronze statue of the poet standing outside.

Morales is one of the poets after whom the Paseo de los Poetas in Puerto de las Nieves was named. The other two are his contemporaries, Alonso Quesada and Saulo Torón.

From the top of the town, a road leads past neatly cultivated vegetable gardens on the valley slopes to **Los Tilos de Moya**, a 91-hectare (225-acre) nature reserve – although it is laurels, not *tilos* (limes), that are protected here. Swathes of them once cloaked the island but few remain, and the protection order has been placed in an attempt to re-establish them.

ARUCAS

Unless you want to visit the centre of the island, retrace your route to the GC-2 motorway and take the turning to **Arucas ㉑**. The **Casco Histórico** has been declared of historic and cultural interest and is best explored on foot. Once you enter the town, find a space at the free open parking area beneath the huge lava-stone church of **San Juan Bautista** (daily 9.30am–12.30pm,

Arucas old town

4.30–7pm; free). Begun in 1909, it is said to owe its inspiration to Antoni Gaudí's Sagrada Família in Barcelona, and there are some similar Modernista flourishes. Inside, it is more conventionally neo-Gothic, and has three splendid rose windows.

From here, wander through the cobbled streets past stone-built buildings, charming squares and open-air cafés towards the Parque Municipal, a shady spot full of exotic trees and plants. In the nearby Calle León y Castillo, a statue of the poet Domingo Rivero, book in hand, stands in front of a giant cactus outside the Casa de Cultura. Rivero, great-uncle of Tomás Morales, was born here in 1852. Inside, leading off a pleasant courtyard with a dragon tree, are much-frequented reading rooms for adults and children.

Near to Arucas, **Montaña de Arucas** is where the Indigenous leader, Doramas, was killed in single-handed combat by Pedro de Vera in 1480. His followers are said to have leapt to their deaths in the *barranco* rather than surrender. Today, there's an observation point here.

Within a five-minute drive of town, the **Ron Arehucas Rum Distillery and Museum** (www.arehucas.es; Mon–Fri 9am–2pm) is considered one of the emblematic buildings of Arucas thanks to its rich rum-making heritage. The **Jardín de la Marquesa** (www.jardindelamarquesa.com) is also worth a visit, with its immaculate peacock-speckled gardens wrapping around a palatial basalt-stone house.

Elsewhere, **Hacienda la Rekompensa** (www.haciendalarekompensa.es; Sun–Fri 10am–5pm; charge) is a traditional banana plantation open for tours and tastings, along with an interesting museum dedicated to the humble fruit. From its cultivation in Papua New Guinea to becoming the main Canarian agricultural export, the highly treasured bounty is transformed into everything from jams to wines.

FIRGAS AND THE FINCA DE OSORIO

From Arucas, there are two routes to Teror. The longer one, on the GC-300, will take you via the pleasant little town of **Firgas**, where a man-made waterfall cascades 30m (90ft) down shallow steps in the centre of a pedestrianized street. Firgas is known for its water. There's a natural spring south of the town and the remarkably tasty product is bottled and sold all over the island. The more direct route is on the GC-43, which will take you past the **Finca de Osorio** (closed to the public), used as an *Aula de la Naturaleza* – a place where students come to learn about conservation, wildlife and agriculture.

TEROR

Teror ㉒ is a delightful little town with some of the best examples of colonial-style architecture you will find outside Las Palmas de Gran Canaria. Carved wooden balconies adorn sugar-white facades, and huge doors open onto fern-filled courtyards. It is also the home of Virgen del Pino (Madonna of the Pine Tree). In 1481, as the island was being subdued by the forces of Pedro de Vera, local shepherds are said to have had a vision of the Virgin appearing to them at the top of a pine tree. The miraculous apparition gave rise to a cult, and today the town has a clutch of lovely churches dedicated to the

Colonial-style Teror

Virgin. In the centre stands the **Basilica de Nuestra Señora del Pino** (Mon–Fri 11am–3pm, Sat–Sun 11am–2.30pm; free), begun in 1767, where the richly clothed statue of the Virgin is displayed, surrounded by votive gifts and symbols. The Virgin del Pino is perhaps the best-loved saint on the island and pilgrims flock to Teror all year round, but especially on her feast day, 8 September. A huge festival is held during that week, with traditional music and dancing and plenty of cheerful secular celebrations accompanying sombre religious rituals.

> ## Indigenous sculptures
>
> At the eastern entrance to Gáldar, a sculpture represents three Indigenous princesses. Another sculpture in the town depicts Tenesor Semidan, the Chief who was forced to accept baptism and collaborate with the Spanish.

Behind the church are stalls selling local produce – homemade bread, cheese and vegetables – as well as religious items. In front stands the Palacio Episcopal (Bishop's Palace), which now houses a cultural centre. On the right-hand side of the basilica is the **Casa Museo de los Patronos de la Virgen del Pino** (tel: 928 630 239; Sun–Fri 11am–6pm) in a beautiful building, set around a courtyard and furnished in the style of a noble, seventeenth-century home. It belongs, as it always has, to the Manrique de Lara family, who still spend the festival week here. At the back of the house are an old bakery and a stable block, where Don Manrique's polished 1951 Triumph shares space with sedan chairs, carts and carriages.

There is a smaller square close by, the **Plaza Teresa de Bolívar**, with a stone fountain in the centre. It is named after the first wife of Simón de Bolívar, the man who led the liberation of many of the Spanish colonies in South America in the nineteenth century.

Roque Nublo and
Roque Bentaiga

Her family came from Teror; his from Tenerife. The couple met
in Venezuela, but Teresa sadly died less than a year after they
were married.

The centre of Teror is closed to traffic, so you can wander
through the cobbled alleys and little squares and drink in the
atmosphere without being disturbed by noise or fumes. If you
come on Sunday morning you will also be able to enjoy the busy,
and very local, market.

THE CENTRAL PEAKS

In order to appreciate the age and majesty of the planet and
the relative insignificance of human beings, all you need is a trip
to the central peaks of Gran Canaria. Over millions of years, the
rocky landscape has been moulded into strange shapes by volcanic eruptions, fierce winds and driving rain, and erosion has also

scored deep *barrancos* (gorges) that plummet to the coast, their fertile soil supporting lush vegetation.

The highest summits are Pico de las Nieves (Peak of the Snows) at 1949m (6394ft), followed by Roque Nublo (Rock of Clouds), at 1803m (5915ft), and Roque Bentaiga (1412m/4632ft). Beneath them, mountain villages cling to the sheer rock, and narrow terraces are cultivated wherever possible. Much of the central pocket of the island is protected as part of the Parque Rural del Nublo; and the land to the west of Artenara forms the Parque Natural de Tamadaba.

While the mountains lure intrepid climbers and serious walkers to their challenging contours, there is a network of relatively short and easy walks that can be made amid stunning scenery, some of them on the historic *caminos reales* (see page 89), others on newer paths.

The central region can be reached quite easily from most parts of the island: direct from Las Palmas de Gran Canaria; from the northern towns of Arucas and Moya; from Agüimes in the east; or from the southern resorts, via the Barranco de Fataga. It is only from the wild and untamed west coast, where tracks either peter out altogether or challenge even the toughest of vehicles and most confident of drivers, that the peaks prove inaccessible.

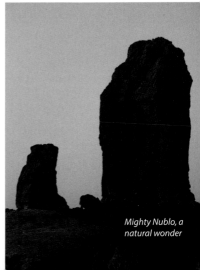

Mighty Nublo, a natural wonder

Parador Hotel de Cruz de Tejeda

If you're approaching from Las Palmas de Gran Canaria, you can take the Santa Brígida road through **Vega de San Mateo** (usually known simply as San Mateo) and up the tortuous road to Tejeda, where bus drivers sound their horns as they approach every sharp bend. Or you could avoid the stress and take bus No. 303, changing in Vega de San Mateo.

This colourful little town has a large food and craft market on Sunday and charming shops full of farm-fresh food and artisanal products. As the road climbs upwards, the lush vegetation changes. If you visit in spring or early summer, you will notice rampaging nasturtiums, blossoming lavender bushes and neat orange groves on the first part of the journey.

Next come the prickly pear cactus *(Opuntia ficus indica)* eucalyptus trees and century plants *(Agave)*, before the entire hillside turns yellow with broom and, close to the top, the pines and holm oaks begin.

CRUZ DE TEJEDA

The top of the pass, at 1580m (5184ft), is marked by a sombre, stone crucifix, the **Cruz de Tejeda** ㉓. Surrounded by towering peaks, this is a hive of commercial activity, with bustling restaurants (one, *El Refugio*, is also a hotel; www.hotelruralelrefugio. com), a shop selling local food specialities, and a row of stalls piled with everything from embroidered tablecloths to dried fruit and local cheeses.

Behind the cross stands a hotel, the beautifully renovated four-star **Parador Hotel de Cruz de Tejeda** (see page 149; www.paradores.es/es/parador-de-cruz-de-tejeda), designed in the 1930s by Néstor Martín-Fernández de la Torre. Magnificent panoramic views can be enjoyed from the hotel, as well as spa and fitness facilities. The view is dominated by the impressive, pointing finger of **Roque Nublo** ㉔, which will have been visible for some time. Depending on the weather and the time of day, the volcanic monolith appears to change colour and it is not hard to understand why the Indigenous peoples revered this rock formation as a holy place. *A camino real* leads from Cruz de Tejeda to Roque Nublo, but there is a shorter walk from Ayacata.

On a clear morning, especially, there is a breathtaking view across the entire island. Away in the distance,

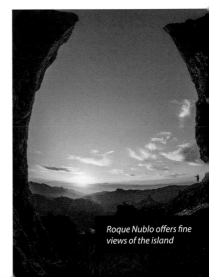

Roque Nublo offers fine views of the island

Tenerife's Mt Teide, snow-capped for much of the year, seems to rise straight out of the sea.

ARTENARA

It is a challenging but beautiful drive from Tejeda to **Artenara** ㉕, which, at an altitude of 1270m (4167ft), is the highest village on the island. It also one of the oldest, pre-dating the Spanish conquest, and Artenara is its Indigenous name. Many of the houses in the village are built into the solid rock, although some of them, with their painted facades, look like ordinary houses, and most have modern amenities.

The cave church, **La Ermita de la Cuevita**, is only identified by a bell above the door. It houses the *Virgen de la Cuevita,* whose festival is celebrated at the end of August. The Iglesia de San Matías is a more conventional church. **Mirador La Cilla** (see page 120) is on most visitors' itineraries, a cave restaurant entered via a long tunnel. It has a sunny terrace with magnificent views of Roque Bentaiga and Roque Nublo, and the hearty island dishes – including *ropa vieja* (beef and tomato stew) *papas arrugadas* (wrinkled potatoes) and grilled meats – are good value.

Close to Artenara, the UNESCO World Heritage Site of **Risco Caído and the Sacred Mountains** nods to a thriving pre-Hispanic culture. Risco Caído (www.riscocaido.grancanaria.com) is a troglodyte-era settlement of cave dwellings, granaries and ceremonial temples (*almogarénes*), tucked into the folds of the cragged volcanic landscape. Rock art scrawled across the caverns' walls hints at occult

Virgin's gifts

A sensible sign in the Basilica de Nuestra Señora del Pino reads: 'Although the Virgin is grateful for your gifts and candles she would rather you gave your money to the poor.'

Pinar de Tamadaba

or religious beliefs. The visitors' centre in Artenara has a replica of one of the caves, or it is possible to strike out from here on one of the many hiking trails for fine views of Risco Caído; the five-mile hike skirting the northern edge of the Caldera de Tejeda or the longer route via Roque Nublo are two of the best. To reach the archeological site, walk along the left bank of the lower course of Barranco Hondo; the 21 caves honeycomb the cliffs around 100 metres above the riverbed.

PINAR DE TAMADABA

From Artenara, a road leads around the **Pinar de Tamadaba** ㉖, 8 sq km (3 sq miles) of protected forest within a much larger nature park, where Canary pines (*Pinus canariensis*) grow to enormous heights, untroubled by pollution – some reach almost 60m (190ft). Forest fires occur periodically, but the pine is capable of rapid regeneration. There are footpaths cleaving through the

Mountain liqueurs

The mountain regions specialize in liqueurs. *Guindilla* is a cherry liqueur made in San Bartolomé and takes its name from the Spanish word for morello cherries – *guindas*. *Mejunje* is a sweet concoction of rum, honey and lemon that was traditionally served to priests when they visited their parishioners.

forest, but great care must be taken not to cause fires or in any way damage the environment. The road does not lead beyond the *pinar*, so you have to return the way you came.

BARRANCO DE FATAGA

If you are approaching the central peaks from the south, you should take the Fataga road from Playa del Inglés. This route leads through the beautiful **Barranco de Fataga**, where burnished walls of rock are reminiscent of canyons in the American West.

After an easy start, the bends in the road become tighter and the valley turns greener. Palm trees line the roadside and tropical fruits are cultivated on the valley floor. Nearby, the village of **Fataga** is perched precipitously on a rock jutting out into the gorge. There is a nice church and several cheerful restaurants, some of them offering barbecues and live music, catering to visitors on jeep safaris from the coast.

The road from here winds towards **San Bartolomé de Tirajana** **27**, a historic little town, the administrative centre of a region that includes Maspalomas and Playa del Inglés. The town's main source of income is the production of fruit, especially cherries.

The Ayuntamiento (Town Hall) has an attractive inner courtyard, and there are two churches – the Neoclassical San Bartolomé, outside which a market is held on Sunday morning, and Santiago el Apóstol. The festival of Santiago (St James) is a major event on 25 July. You may want to stop at the petrol station here to ensure you have a full tank, as garages are few and far between in the mountains.

PICO DE LAS NIEVES AND ROQUE BENTAIGA

Following signs to Tejeda, you will reach the little village of **Ayacata**, from where there is a popular and fairly undemanding walk to Roque Nublo, which takes about forty minutes each way. It passes another, smaller rock figure known as El Fraile (The Monk). If you look carefully, you may (just) see a resemblance to a praying monk.

Off to the right, a road wriggles round a reservoir, the Presa de los Hornos. Not far away is the **Degollada de Bercerra** (daily 10am–5pm; free), an information centre with a *mirador* offering panoramic views. Looming above is the **Pico de las Nieves ㉘**, the

highest peak on the island, crowned by a radar station and tv transmitter. The summit is not accessible as it is used as a military base, but there is a lookout point not far below.

The road to the west from Ayacata, signposted to Bentaiga, is asphalted at first but soon becomes a gravel track. After Roque Nublo, **Roque Bentaiga** is the most spectacular monolith in the mountain range. In 1483, it was the site of a fierce battle in which the Spaniards, led

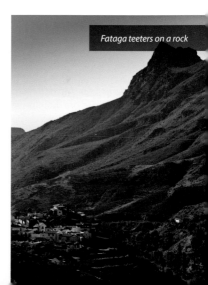

Fataga teeters on a rock

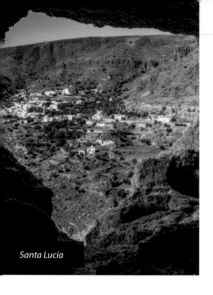

Santa Lucía

by Pedro de Vera, defeated the Indigenous people. An Indigenous refuge, called the Cueva del Rey (King's Cave), is huddled at the foot of the outcrop.

It is well worth stopping at the **Centro de Interpretación** (daily 10am–4pm, Sat–Sun until 6pm; hours unpredictable in winter) to get some background information. From here, those with enough energy can scramble the last stretch to the peak.

FORTALEZA GRANDE AND SANTA LUCÍA

An alternative way to approach the central peaks is from the east, from Agüimes, via Santa Lucía on the GC-550 or from the Cruce de Sardina exit off the motorway (GC-65). It almost goes without saying that these are winding roads with sharp bends, but the scenery is spectacular, with prickly pears, euphorbia and olive trees gradually losing ground to bare, reddish rock.

Off to the left of the GC-65, you will see **Fortaleza Grande**, a rock uncannily shaped like a castle, which was one of the last refuges of the Indigenous peoples. Some of those who survived the defeat at Roque Bentaiga obeyed the command of their leader, Tenesor Semidan, to surrender; others, it is said, threw themselves from these cliffs.

La Fortaleza Interpretation Center (www.lafortaleza.es; Tues–Sun 10am–5pm; charge) has a modern exhibition hall, a central courtyard for workshops and events, an audiovisual room with a short documentary detailing the everyday lives of pre-Hispanic villagers and a viewing terrace with information boards on the local environment and a reproduction of an Indigenous dwelling.

Surrounded by pine trees, **Santa Lucía** ㉙ is a beautiful little village with blindingly white houses, clouds of bougainvillaea tumbling over walls, and an imposing domed church crowned by a double belltower. There's a children's playground and a small museum, the **Museo Castillo de la Fortaleza** (daily 10.30am–5pm) where Indigenous artefacts, agricultural tools and a Roman amphora are displayed.

A final way to approach the central peaks is via Moya or Arucas in the north. The road from Arucas is the better-maintained of the two options, but the Moya route wends past the lovely Pinos de Gáldar pine forest. Both lead – circuitously, of course – to Cruz de Tejeda.

CAMINOS REALES

A series of ancient paths known as *caminos reales* – royal paths – has been restored and opened up to walkers as part of an attempt to promote conservation-conscious tourism and *senderismo* – hiking. These old tracks, once the only means of navigating the interior of Gran Canaria, centre on Cruz de Tejeda and radiate out to much of the island, from Maspalomas in the south to Agaete in the northwest. While some walks are demanding, others are relatively short and gentle. For more information, contact the Turismo de Gran Canaria, Calle Triana 93, Las Palmas de Gran Canaria or find information and download maps for hiking routes online (www.grancanaria.com).

Gran Canaria has excellent
conditions for windsurfing

THINGS TO DO

SPORTS

The spectrum of sports and outdoor activities available on Gran Canaria runs from the mildly energetic to the extremely vigorous. Activities take place on, in or under the water, while others are land-based pursuits, such as hiking, cycling, running, horse riding and golf. No wonder, then, that Gran Canaria is often referred to as an open-air gym and has a year-round calendar of sport tournaments and international events.

SURFING AND PADDLEBOARDING

Gran Canaria is considered one of the best places in the world for windsurfing – some say only Hawaii beats it. It can be practised all along the coast running from Melenera in the east to Maspalomas in the south. At **Playa de Vargas** and **Pozo Izquierdo** near Arinaga, strong winds are constant year-round and waves always high. A little further south, near San Agustín, winds are good in Bahía Feliz and Playa del Águila.

The two best windsurf schools, which offer beginners' and advanced courses, are **Fanatic Boarders Center** (Playa de Trajalillo, Urbanización Bahía Feliz; www.fbcgrancanaria.com) and **BD Surf School** (Playa del Águila, San Agustín and Playa del Ingles; tel: 928 767 999, www.surfbd.com), run by record-holding 42-time world champion Björn Dunkerbeck. Windsurfing conditions are also decent at Playa de las Canteras, Las Palmas de Gran Canaria and Gáldar in the far northwest corner.

The north of the island, between Las Palmas de Gran Canaria and Gáldar, is best for surfing and bodyboarding. Constant onshore winds along this rocky coastline make ideal conditions

Boat trips

To experience the sea while someone else does the work, take a trip in a glass bottom boat run by Líneas Salmon (tel: 649 919 383, www.lineassalmon.es) or Líneas Bluebird (tel: 629 989 633/366, www.lineasbluebird. com) between the ports of Arguineguín, Puerto Rico and Puerto de Mogán. Or try the Afrikat from Puerto Rico (tel: 637 564 679, www. afrikat.com) for a lazy day on a sailing catamaran, with on-board food and drink.

for surfers, and waves can reach up to 5m (16ft) high. Conditions are good around Arinaga, on the east coast, and between Playa del Inglés and Maspalomas in the south, where tuition and courses are offered by **PR Surfing** (Av. de Moya no. 6, C.C Eurocenter loc 80, Maspolomas; tel: 628 104 025, www.prsurfing.com).

Stand-up paddleboarding at Playa de las Canteras in Las Palmas de Gran Canaria is a great way to glide across the sea on calm days. There are a number of reliable paddleboarding outfits, including Mojo Surf (www.mojosurf.es), Brisa School (www.brisaschool. com) and Oceanside Surf School (www.grancanariasurf.es).

DEEP-SEA DIVING

There is a fascinating world beneath the waters off Gran Canaria and a number of excellent diving sites. In Las Palmas de Gran Canaria, where La Barra forms a giant aquarium protected from the force of the waves, there is a wealth of underwater life. On the east coast at **Playa del Cabrón**, the diversity of fish and vegetation is so great that the area has been designated a marine reserve. **Pasito Blanco**, in the south near **Puerto Rico**, is another good spot, with ideal conditions for underwater photography, plus two wrecks offshore ripe for exploration (experienced divers only). In the northwest, **Sardina** is a popular spot for night dives into rocky depths of 17m (52ft).

Reputable diving schools with qualified instructors include: **Buceo Canarias Medusasub** (Calle Joaquin Blanco Torrent opposite dock H, Las Palmas de Gran Canaria; tel: 928 232 085, www.buceocanarias.com); **Zeus Dive Center** (Hotel IFA Continental, Av Italia 2, Playa del Ingles; tel: 689 082 298, www.zeusdivecenter.com); **Davy Jones Diving** (Calle Luis Velasco 36-38, Playa de Arinaga, Aguimes; tel: 928 180 840, www.davyjonesdiving.com); and **Gran Canaria Divers** (Calle la Puntillo 3; tel: 928 948 424, www.grancanariadivers.com). Free pick-up and drop-off between accommodation and dive sites is often included in the price.

SAILING

Gran Canaria is a sailor's dream, especially from April to October. Winds are reliably good, and the climate is excellent. The main centres are Las Palmas de Gran Canaria and the south coast, specifically Pasito Blanco, Arguineguín, Puerto Rico and Puerto de Mogán. The island attracts experienced sailors – members of Puerto Rico's sailing school have brought home several Olympic gold medals – but it suits beginners too.

The annual Atlantic Rally for Cruisers (ARC; www.worldcruising.com) kicks off at the Muelle Deportivo in Las Palmas de Gran Canaria and embarks on the 2700-nautical mile journey to St Lucia in the Caribbean.

Gran Canaria is a diving hotspot

Sailing enthusiasts flock to the south coast

Traditionally, it was celebrated in October, but due to high demand, a January date has been added to the itinerary.

Among many reliable sailing clubs and schools are: **Real Club Náutico**, Calle León y Castillo 308, Las Palmas de Gran Canaria, tel: 928 234 566, www.rcngc.com; **Real Club Victoria**, Paseo de las Canteras 4, tel: 928 460 630, www.realclubvictoria.com; **AIS TraC**, Juan Deniz 10, Puerto Mogan, tel: 622 170 018, www.aistrac.com; and the **ICI-Sailing Club**, Calle Leon y Castillo 308, tel: 407 501 014, www.ici-sailing.org. For lateen sailing, contact the **Federación de Vela Latina Canaria**, Muelle Deportivo, Las Palmas de Gran Canaria, tel: 928 230 616, www.federacionvelalatinadebotes.com.

DEEP-SEA FISHING

Gran Canaria is well known for its game fishing, and Pasito Blanco, Puerto Rico and Puerto de Mogán are the major centres. Puerto Rico's fishermen are the proud holders of numerous world records in deep-sea fishing, but this is a sport in which beginners can take part too. Several varieties of tuna and marlin as well as swordfish and sometimes sharks can be found in these well-stocked waters. The deep-sea fishing season is roughly from May to September, but there is bottom-fishing available year-round.

A number of organizations offer fishing trips that include lunch and equipment; try **White Striker** (Puerto Rico; tel: 610 480 760, www.whitestriker.com) with a knowledgeable skipper. Those who don't want to fish can relax on the solarium at the front of the boat. Tuna is sold direct to restaurants; marlin is collected by staff from a children's home in Las Palmas de Gran Canaria. Also recommended in Puerto Rico is **Cavalier & Blue Marlin 3** (tel: 607 626 237, www. bluemarlin3.com).

There are four main game-fishing tournaments a year: July is bookended by the Corona Cup and Puerto Rico Tournament, both in Puerto Rico, while the Pasito Blanco Tournament is at the end of August and Las Palmas Tournament is in October (www.grancanaria.com).

ANCIENT SPORTS

Lucha Canaria – Canary Islands wrestling – is the most popular traditional sport on the islands and can be seen at rural fiestas, in the Estadio López Socas in Las Palmas de Gran Canaria, and in Gáldar. Two teams of twelve wrestlers take it in turns to face a member of the opposing team in a sandy ring, with the aim of throwing the opponent to the ground. After a maximum of three rounds (*bregas*), the winner is the team that loses the fewest wrestlers. The game was practised in pre-Hispanic times, when it may have had more serious overtones.

Juego del palo (stick fighting) is another ancient rural sport, also practised at fiestas. The object is to move the body as little as possible while attacking and fending off the blows of an opponent.

WALKING, RUNNING AND SWIMMING

There's lots to do on land, and the most popular activity is hiking – *senderismo*. This is being promoted by the Cabildo Insular as a way of diversifying the tourist industry and encouraging visitors to explore the island's interior. More than 66,000 hectares (164,000 acres) of land in Gran Canaria is under a protection order. There are rural parks, nature reserves, fully protected reserves and natural monuments, most granting public access. A series of ancient paths, the *caminos reales*, or royal paths (see page 89), once the only means of traversing much of the island, has been opened up for walkers. There are challenging walks and climbs in the mountainous centre of the island, but there are many other less strenuous routes as well. A guidebook to these paths can be bought in the bookshop of the **Cabildo Insular de Gran Canaria** (Calle Cano 24, Las Palmas de Gran Canaria). Or contact the Turismo de Gran Canaria (Calle Triana 93, Las Palmas de Gran Canaria; tel: 928 219 600, www.grancanaria. com), which publishes a series of leaflets, including maps.

There are many great walks in the *barrancos*. For general information on organized hikes, contact **Grupo Montañero Gran Canaria** (Calle Guillermo Santana Rivero 1, Las Palmas de Gran Canaria; tel: 928 427 475, www.gmgrancanaria.es). For hikes with a knowledgeable guide, contact **Hiking World** (Plaza Tiscamanita, Maspolomas; tel: 654 588 038, www.hikingworldgrancanaria.com). Visit www. visitaguimes.com for walking routes and trails in the Barranco de Guayadeque and other suggested routes.

A couple of hiking events worth considering include the Gran Canaria Walking Festival, a five-day ramble in October, or Transgrancanaria, a three-day ultra-trail race across the island in March. Artenara Trail is also popular, with two events in June. Gran Canaria Maspalomas Marathon is in November, or triathletes might prefer the Swimrun Maspalomas in June or Challenge Mogán in April (www.grancanaria.com).

CYCLING

Gran Canaria is a mecca for cyclists thanks to year-round warm weather, varied terrain, and abundant flora and fauna. From scenic coastal routes to long-distance trails and mountain-biking adventures, the island has something for everyone. For mountain bikers, some of the most challenging climbs include the CI-12-6 to La Culata, the mettle-testing 25km ride to Roque Nublo and the gruelling 12km ascent in the Valley of the Tears – though the views are ample reward for the shaking quads. As fifty percent of the island is a UNESCO World Biosphere Reserve, you won't be short of scenic surrounds en route: spot birds of prey swooping above mountains or lizards scuttling in the undergrowth. **Bike Center Freemotion** (www.free-motion.com) offers bike rentals and cycling tours, while **Cycle Gran Canaria** (www.cyclegrancanaria.com) arranges cycling

Maspalomas Golf Club

holidays, from a six-day guided island tour to a seven-night mountain-biking sojourn.

Competitive cyclists should sign up for Transgrancanaria Bike in November or Gran Canaria Bike Week in December.

GOLF

Gran Canaria has a strong golfing tradition and is home to several PGA Championship golf courses. **Real Club de Golf de Las Palmas** (Santa Brígida; tel: 928 351 050, www.realclubdegolfdelaspalmas. com), with 18 holes, par 71, is draped across the rim of the Bandama volcanic crater and is the oldest club in Spain, founded by British expats in 1891. The 18-hole, par-73 **Maspalomas Golf Club** (Avda TTOO Neckermann s/n; tel: 928 762 581, www.maspalomasgolf.net) is generally flat, with its ninth hole by the dunes; it is also the first

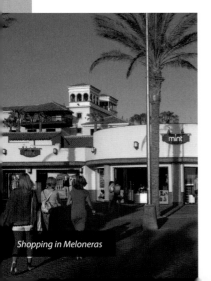

pay-and-play golf course in Spain. **Salobre Golf Club** (Autopista GC-1; tel: 928 943 000, www.salobrehotel. com) has two Arizona-style courses (north and south). Ocean views abound at the 18-hole, par-71 **Meloneras Golf Club** (GC-500, s/n; tel: 928 14 53 09; www.melonerasgolf.es), while the 18-hole, par-72 **Anfi Tauro Golf** (Valle de Tauro, s/n, tel: 928 560 462, www.anfi. com) is the perfect blend of natural and man-made landscapes. Visit www.gran canaria.com for details.

Shopping in Meloneras

HORSE RIDING

The **Real Club de Golf** at Santa Brígida (tel: 928 351 050, www.real clubdegolfdelaspalmas.com) has a riding school. Lessons and trekking are also available at the **Picadero Oasis de Maspalomas** (tel: 928 762 378) and **El Salobre Canyon Horse Farm** (Maspalomas; tel: 616 418 363, www.elsalobrehr.es), which arranges pick-ups from the southern resorts.

FLYING, PARACHUTING AND SKY DIVING

To try flying or parachuting, contact the **Escuela Canaria de Parapente** (tel: 626 331 588, www.parapentegrancanaria.com), or the **Club de Parapente Sirocco** (tel: 696 860 216) in Las Palmas de Gran Canaria. For sky diving – a flight over the Maspalomas dunes and a jump in tandem with an instructor from 3000m (9840ft) – contact **Paraclub Gran Canaria** (tel: 928 157 000, www.iJump.es).

STARGAZING

Gran Canaria, with its dark skies and lack of light pollution, is a certified Starlight Destination. **AstroGC** (www.astrogc.com) offers stargazing excursions to the western mountains, with astronomer-led talks and large-aperture telescopes, while **Astroeduca** (www.astroeduca.com) hosts astronomical evenings at dedicated viewpoints. If you'd prefer to go solo, *miradores astronómicos* around the island offer the best chance to spot constellations, nebulas and other celestial gems.

SHOPPING

Gran Canaria looks set to maintain its status as a Free Trade Zone for the foreseeable future, despite membership of the EU, and taxes (IGIC) are low, at seven percent, so there are savings to be made on tobacco, spirits, perfume, cosmetics, watches, jewellery, and electronic and optical equipment in Las Palmas de Gran Canaria

A colourful stall at Vegueta food market

duty-free shops. Handicraft items (*artesanía*), including textiles, baskets and ceramics, can be found in shops and markets all over the island, but the best-quality goods are sold in the outlets of the **Fundación para la Etnografía y el Desarrollo de la Artesanía Canaria** (FEDAC; www.fedac.org). The main one is at Calle Domingo J. Navarro 7, Las Palmas de Gran Canaria. FEDAC shops also sell the *cuchillos canarios (*knives) once used by banana workers and shepherds, which have now become collectors' items.

Calle Peregrina in Las Palmas de Gran Canaria is peppered with attractive little boutiques and galleries. The **Librería del Cabildo Insular** (the official government bookshop; Calle Cano 24, Las Palmas de Gran Canaria; tel: 928 381 539, www.libroscanarios.org) is the place for maps and books about all the Canary Islands.

In the big commercial zones of Las Palmas de Gran Canaria, you will find all the major stores. The biggest centres in and around Las Palmas de Gran Canaria are **Las Arenas** near the Auditorio Kraus; **Alisios** on Calle Hermanos Domínguez Santana; and the largest Spanish department store, **El Corte Inglés** in the **Avenida Mesa y López**, which is known as a *zona comercial*. Mega-complex **El Muelle** is on the Muelle Santa Catalina. In Puerto Rico, **Mogan Mall** is packed with all the usual high store and designer brands.

Among edible items, *queso de flor*, the famous cheese made in Guía, is a good choice. The cheeses can be tasted and bought at the

Santa María Guía factory and at farmers' markets around the island. Jars of mojo sauce and *bienmesabe* (almond dessert) are also ideal.

MARKETS

Most towns have a weekly market, selling food, flowers and household goods. There's a good one in **Puerto de Mogán** (Friday and Monday) and another in the San Fernando district of **Playa del Inglés** (Wednesday and Saturday). **San Mateo** has a huge farmers' market on Sunday morning. In Las Palmas de Gran Canaria, the slightly overpriced **Vegueta** food market is a riot of colours and scents every morning except Sunday, and is surrounded by tiny, white-tiled bars. **Mercado del Puerto** (Calle Albareda; daily) offers fresh produce at bargain prices.

NIGHTLIFE

Very little happens before midnight, so a quiet place you pass at 10.30pm may be popping two hours later. In Las Palmas de Gran Canaria, Plaza de España in the Mesa y López district is lively. **Ginger** on Paseo de las Canteras is the perfect place to sit with a mojito overlooking the beach. Further south, the café tables in Plaza Hurtado de Mendoza are full till the early hours. Here, **La Azotea de Benito** (www. lazoteadebenito.com) boasts wonderful views from its roof terrace. There is a rich nightlife in Playa del Inglés and Maspalomas, too. **Chinawhite** in Maspalomas (Avenida de Espana 7; www.chinawhite-grancanaria.com) is popular

Unusual plants

The Gando airport shop has a wide selection of plants, from miniature dragon trees to *strelitzia* (bird of paradise) flowers, as well as a variety of seeds. Whether or not they will grow in the English climate is a gamble, but they make unusual gifts – and there is no restriction on bringing them into the UK.

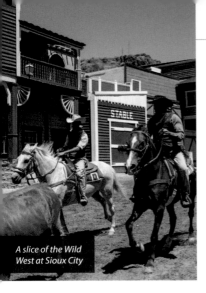

A slice of the Wild West at Sioux City

and has a good rota of international DJs. A firm favourite, **Iguazú Lounge** in Playa des Ingles (Avenida Tirajana) has a reputation for the best cocktails in the area. The **Yumbo Centre** is known for its gay bars and clubs (www.yumbocentrum.com).

For a flutter, try Casino Las Palmas in the capital (Calle Simon Bolivar 3; tel: 928 234 882, www.casinolaspalmas.com) or the Gran Casino in Meloneras (Calle Mar Mediterráneo 1; tel: 928 143 909, www.grancasinocostameloneras.com). From casinos to classical, the **Auditorio Alfredo Kraus** at the far end of Las Canteras beach (www.auditorioteatrolaspalmasgc.es) presents music recitals by the resident Gran Canaria Philharmonic and visiting orchestras and top-class soloists. The **Teatro Cuyás** (Calle Viera y Clavijo s/n, Triana; www.teatrocuyas.com) stages world and classical music, dance and theatre, as does **Teatro Pérez Galdós** (Plaza Stagno 1; www.auditorioteatrolaspalmasgc.es) and **Teatro Guiniguada** (Calle Mesa de León 2, Las Palmas de Gran Canaria). **CICCA** (Alameda de Colón 1; tel: 928 368 687, www.lacajadecanarias.es) has a varied programme of films, music, modern dance and theatre.

CHILDREN'S GRAN CANARIA

Gran Canaria is a great place for kids, with plenty to do beyond the beach. Close to Playa del Inglés/Maspalomas you will find:

Aqualand (daily 10am–5pm), Carretera Palmitos Park Km3, tel: 928 140 525, www.aqualand.es. The biggest waterpark in the Canaries, with slides and flumes of all descriptions.

Palmitos Park (daily 10am–5pm), Barranco de Palmitos s/n, tel: 928 797 070, www.palmitospark.es. The sister of nearby Aqualand (money-saving joint tickets available) is home to birds of prey, parrots, fish, reptiles and much more.

Hangar 37 (Tues–Fri 3–8pm, Sat–Sun 10am–8pm), Carretera General del Sur GC-50 Km45, tel: 669 829 233, www.hangar37.es. Large airsoft battlefield and a shooting gallery; new mission every 10min so no need to reserve, just turn up and join the existing game.

Holiday World (daily 4–11pm), Maspalomas, tel: 928 730 498, www.holidayworldmaspalomas.com. Another huge leisure park with an escape room and other cool adventures.

Sioux City (Tues–Sun 10am–5pm, Fri BBQ 8pm), Cañon del Águila, San Agustín, tel: 928 762 573, www.parquetematicosiouxcitypark.com. A Wild West park with gunfights and bank hold-ups.

Submarine Adventure (daily 10am–5pm), Puerto de Mogán, tel: 928 565 108, www.atlantidasubmarine.com. A 90-minute voyage to the bottom of the sea in a yellow submarine.

Cocodrilo Park (Fri–Sun 10.30am–4.30pm, daily at peak times), Los Corralillos, Agüimes, tel: 928 784 725, www.cocodriloparkzoo.com. Parrots, monkeys, deer, plus some three hundred crocodiles.

Guagua Turística (daily), Las Palmas de Gran Canaria. Children love a trip around town on the open-topped hop-on-hop-off bus.

Museo Elder (Tues–Thurs 9.30am–7.30pm, Fri–Sun 10am–8pm) www.museoelder.org. Huge science and tech museum in Parque Santa Catalina with a dedicated kids' section and an IMAX cinema.

Acuario Poema del Mar (9.30am–5.30pm), Av de los Consignatarios, s/n, tel: 928 010 350, www.poema-del-mar.com. Get up close and personal with the weird and wonderful creatures of the Atlantic at Snapú Dock's amazing aquarium.

WHAT'S ON

6 January: Epifanía del Señor (Epiphany). Children receive their Christmas presents. In Las Palmas de Gran Canaria the Three Kings (Los Reyes) ride into town, throwing sweets to the crowd.

February: Fiesta de Almendros (Almond Blossom Festival) in Tejeda and Valsequillo (date varies). Traditional handicrafts, dance and sports displays.

Late February/early March: Carnival. Celebrations are particularly outrageous in Las Palmas de Gran Canaria and Playa del Inglés.

April: Semana Santa. The week preceding Easter is a time of solemn processions. Also International Film Festival in Las Palmas de Gran Canaria, various locations.

End April to early May: Cheese festival, Santa María de Guía. Traditional dancing and lots of local produce.

Mid-June: Corpus Christi. The streets of Vegueta and the Plaza de Santa Ana in Las Palmas de Gran Canaria, and main squares in Arucas and Gáldar, are carpeted with flowers, grasses and coloured sand.

24 June: San Juan (Feast of St John). Dancing, processions and sporting activities in Artenara, Telde, Las Palmas de Gran Canaria and Arucas.

16 July: Nuestra Señora del Carmen, the patron saint of fishermen, is honoured in all ports, but especially in Arguineguín and Puerto de Mogán. Statues of the Virgin are taken out to sea in processions of decorated boats.

4 August: Bajada de las Ramas (Bringing down the Branches) is held in Agaete and Puerto de las Nieves. The villagers carry branches from the mountains to the sea and whip the waves.

8 September: Virgen del Pino. Important festival in Teror, which is a mixture of religious rituals and secular fun.

11 September: Fiesta del Charco (Festival of the Lagoon) in Puerto de la Aldea, San Nicolás. Participants try to catch fish with their hands, and duck each other into the water.

Second Saturday in October: Fiestas de la Naval (Festival of the Sea). Maritime processions in Las Palmas de Gran Canaria and other ports celebrate the victory of the Armada over the English in 1595.

FOOD AND DRINK

Canary Islands' food has much in common with that of mainland Spain, but with interesting regional differences. There are also dishes similar to those found in parts of Latin America – although whether these recipes were introduced by Canarian emigrants, or American inventions brought back by returnees, is debatable.

Today, a wave of ambitious young chefs is showcasing local ingredients and giving a contemporary spin to traditional recipes, as part of a wider island drive towards sustainability. The culinary efforts are paying off: high-end restaurants are springing up across Gran Canaria, and there are now five Michelin-starred restaurants on the island. Foodies can enjoy a range of immersive gastronomic experiences, visiting local markets, wineries and cheesemakers and touring *fincas* and plantations for a behind-the-scenes glimpse into this thriving farm-to-fork movement.

Salpicón de pescado

FISH

As you would expect on an Atlantic island, there is an abundance of fish and seafood on restaurant menus. Along with the ubiquitous *sardinas*, fresh from the ocean, the fish most commonly chalked up on blackboards are *cherne* (sea bass),

Papas arrugadas con mojo

vieja (parrot fish), *sama* (sea bream) and *bacalao* (salt cod). You will also find *merluza* (hake) *atún* (tuna) and *bonito* (a variety of tuna) and seafood such as *gambas* (prawns), *pulpo* (octopus), *calamares* (squid) and *almejas* (clams).

Often, fish will be served simply grilled along with salad, a drizzle of *mojo* sauce and *papas arrugadas* – a perfectly balanced (and delicious) dish. *Sancocho canario* is a popular recipe, a stew made with red grouper or sea bass, potatoes and yams, spiced up with a hot variety of *mojo* sauce. *Salpicón de pescado* is another dish you will see on many restaurant menus: this is sea bass or grouper cooked, chopped and served cold with a mixture of onions, garlic, tomatoes and peppers, topped with crumbled hard-boiled egg and olives.

A delicacy introduced from the Basque country is *calamares rellenos de bacalao* – small squid with a tasty, cod-based stuffing, sometimes served in a creamy sauce.

MEAT

If you don't like fish, don't despair, there's plenty of meat to be found. *Cabrito* (kid) – sometimes called *baifo* – and *conejo* (rabbit) are most common, but lamb (*cordero*) pork (*cerdo*) and chicken (*pollo*) are popular.

There are also some good steak restaurants. Both goat and rabbit are often served *al salmorejo* (with green peppers, in a herb and garlic marinade). *Chorizo de Teror* is a local speciality – soft, easy-to-spread red spicy sausage.

SOUPS

Most of the world's traditional dishes originated as a way of filling stomachs with what was available and inexpensive. In the Canary Islands, this meant a whole range of substantial soups and stews. *Ropa vieja* ("old clothes") is a mixture of meat, tomatoes and chickpeas; *puchero* includes meat, pumpkin and any vegetables available; while *rancho canario* – mixing vermicelli with chickpeas, potatoes, bacon, chorizo and chicken – is the most elaborate and some say the best.

Many of the soups contain chunks of corn on the cob. Vegetarians should note that even watercress soup (*potaje de berros*), a staple of many menus, could have chunks of bacon in it. And celery soup (*potaje de apio*) may contain scraps of pork.

VEGETABLES

There is an abundance of vegetables on offer year-round, depending on those that are in season. Pulses such as lentils (*lentejas*) and chickpeas (*garbanzos*) bulk out a lot of recipes. Canary tomatoes are delicious; ask for *tomates aliñados*, tomato salad drizzled with olive oil and lashings of garlic, topped with parsley.

Pimientos de padrón – small green peppers cooked whole and covered with salt – originated in Galicia and are now found everywhere. Avocados (strictly speaking a fruit, not a vegetable) are served at a perfect stage of ripeness.

Most dishes are accompanied by potatoes (*papas*), and sometimes by *ñame*, a kind of yam. You'll encounter *papas arrugadas* (wrinkled potatoes), which are served with meat and fish or by themselves as tapas. They are small potatoes cooked in their skins in salted water then dried over a low heat until their skins wrinkle and a salty crust forms. It is said that this dish originated with fishermen who used to boil the potatoes in seawater.

MOJO

Papas arrugadas, and many meat dishes, are usually accompanied by *mojo rojo*, a sauce whose basic ingredients are tomatoes, peppers and paprika. A spicier version (*mojo picón*) contains hot chili

Fresh, seasonal produce is sold year-round

pepper as well. *Mojo verde* is a green sauce made with oil, vinegar, garlic, coriander and parsley, usually served with fish. The sauces arrive at the table in small bowls so you can use as much or as little as you like. Every restaurant – and probably every home – seems to have their own version and entire *mojo* recipe books are published.

Truchas canarias

Trucha is a word to be careful with. It actually means trout, but *truchas canarias* are small pastries filled with sweet potato, almond, lemon zest, sugar and cinnamon.

GOFIO

Made of wheat, barley or a mixture of the two, *gofio* was the staple food of Indigenous people and still forms an essential part of the island diet today – you even see sacks of *gofio para perros* (*gofio* for dogs). The cereal is toasted before being ground into flour, and has a multiplicity of uses. It is stirred into soups and into children's milk and used to thicken sauces. It is made into ice cream and mixed with oil, salt and sugar into a kind of bread, not unlike *polenta*. It is also blended with fish stock to make a thick soup called *gofio escaldado*.

CHEESE, FRUIT AND DESSERTS

Gran Canaria is known for its cheeses made from a blend of goat, cow and sheep milk. The best known is *queso de flor de Guía*, using a mixture of sheep and cow milk curdled with the juice of flowers from the cardoon thistle, and has been awarded a Denomination of Origin. It has also won several World Cheese Awards, as has the *queso tierno de Valsequillo*, a mild, smooth cheese like mozzarella.

Home-grown Canary Island fruit is delicious. As well as the small, local bananas, there are papayas, guavas, mangoes and

Gran Canarian
cheeses are delicious

all types of citrus fruit, incredible by themselves, squeezed into fresh juices and smoothies or used to flavour ice cream.

On many menus, desserts are limited to ice cream (*helado*), *flan* (the ubiquitous caramel custard), fresh fruit – in particular, papaya salad with orange juice – and the one you see everywhere, *bienmesabe*, which translates as 'tastes good to me' – and so it does. It is a mixture of crushed almonds, lemon, sugar (lots), cinnamon and egg yolks.

WHAT TO DRINK

The breakfast drink of choice is coffee. *Café solo* is a small, strong black, like an *espresso*; a *cortado*, served in a glass, is a shot of coffee with a small amount of hot milk; *café con leche* is a large milky coffee. *Café con leche y leche*, a local speciality, is *cortado* with both regular and condensed milk. *Americano* and hot chocolate are also available. Tea is becoming more popular and there are a few places that serve a proper cuppa, though usually you will just get a teabag in a little cup.

You are advised not to drink tap water, but *agua mineral* is sold everywhere – *con gas* is sparkling, *sin gas* is still. *Zumo de naranja*, freshly squeezed orange juice, is widely available. Wine is usually drunk with meals. You will find a great variety of both Spanish wines from the mainland and Canarian varieties in smaller batches.

The award-winning Gran Canaria Wine Route is the only certified wine route in the Canary Islands. It includes family-run wineries holding Denomination of Origin (DOC) status and signature restaurants; see www.rutadelvinodegrancanaria.net for information.

When Arucas had a thriving sugar industry, it also used to be a centre of rum production. There is still a distillery there, the Destileria Arehucas (open for visits; www.arehucas.es), producing excellent rum. The spirit also forms the basis of *Mejunje*, a local drink in which the spirit is blended with honey and lemon. Another speciality is *Guindilla*, the cherry liqueur made in San Bartolomé.

Beer is extremely popular on the island. You will see familiar Spanish brands and other imported beers are available, but the most popular is the locally produced Tropical.

WHERE TO EAT

When it comes to places to eat, the choice is wide. There are upmarket restaurants in Las Palmas de Gran Canaria and in the south that can compete with those in any capital city and are not expensive by northern European standards. There are fishermen's *tavernas* where the fish takes centre stage; and rural *parrillas* – grills – where all kinds of meat are barbecued over an open fire and dished up with generous helpings of *papas arrugadas* and *mojo rojo*.

A *piscolabis* is a snack bar serving sandwiches and light bites. When you see restaurants advertising *cocina casalinga* – home-cooking – you'll usually get inexpensive, typically Canarian food, although the quality, of course, can vary. There are not many places that style themselves as tapas bars, but many middle-of-the-range and inexpensive restaurants offer a selection of tapas, and some of the plates are quite large – two or three would make a meal for most people.

Bars, generally, are places in which to drink, not eat, though most will have pastries to accompany the morning coffee; some may serve sandwiches (*bocadillos*) or tapas. A *kiosco* has the same role and can be found in the main squares of most towns and villages.

WHEN TO EAT

The islanders, like the people of mainland Spain, eat late. It is not unusual to sit down to lunch at three o'clock, and ten o'clock is a relatively early hour to start dinner. Some restaurants may close for a few hours between lunch and dinner, but many serve food all day. Those who cater mostly to foreign visitors, aware that habits are different, will have their lunch menus out by midday and serve dinner as early as you like. Sunday lunch is a major event in Gran Canaria and as this continues throughout the afternoon many restaurants are closed on Sunday evening. Some also close one evening during the week – usually Monday or Tuesday.

Meloneras has an abundance of restaurants, many with sea views

TO HELP YOU ORDER

Could we have a table, please? **¿Nos puede dar una mesa, por favor?**

Excuse me **Perdón**

Do you have a set menu? **¿Tiene un menú del día?**

I would like... **Quisiera…**

The bill, please **La cuenta, por favor**

one/two/three/four **uno/dos/tres/cuatro**

MENU READER

à la plancha grilled
agua mineral mineral water
al ajillo in garlic
arroz rice
asado roast
atún tuna
azúcar sugar
bacalao cod
bocadillo sandwich
boquerones anchovies
buey/res beef
calamares squid
callos tripe
cangrejo crab
cerdo pork
cerveza beer
champiñones mushrooms
cocido stew
cordero lamb
ensalada salad
entremeses hors d'oeuvre
helado ice cream

jamón serrano cured ham
judías beans
langosta lobster
leche milk
mariscos shellfish
mejillones mussels
morcilla black pudding
pan bread
pescado fish
picante spicy
poco hecho rare
pollo chicken
postre dessert
pulpitos baby octopus
queso cheese
sal salt
salsa sauce
ternera veal
tortilla omelette
trucha trout
verduras vegetables
vino wine

WHERE TO EAT

We have used the following symbols to give an idea of the price for a three-course meal for one, including wine, cover and service:

€€€€   **over 60 euros**
€€€   **40–60 euros**
€€   **25–40 euros**
€   **below 25 euros**

LAS PALMAS DE GRAN CANARIA

Bevir €€€ *Pérez Galdós 43, tel: 928 358 548, www.restaurantebevir.com*. This Michelin-listed restaurant serves artfully presented dishes that look as good as they taste. Recipes draw on the natural larder of the land and sea, weaved together in two inventive tasting menus.

De Contrabando €€€ *Calle Fernando Guanarteme 16, tel: 928 228 416, www.decontrabandorestaurante.com*. Innovative fusion cuisine with influences from around the world, served in an elegant Gatsby-style dining space. Scoring a listing in the Michelin guide, dishes are perfect for sharing and paired with excellent Canarian wines.

Deliciosa Marta €€€ *Perez Galdos 33, Las Palmas de Gran Canaria, tel: 928 370 882*. A restaurant with personality in spades, *Deliciosa Marta* serves up Canarian-style, market-inspired cooking with a contemporary flourish. With bare stone walls and wooden ceiling beams, the interiors are as impressive as the cuisine.

Embarcadero €€€ *Club Marítimo Varadero, Muelle Deportivo, tel: 928 233 067, www.restauranteembarcadero.com*. In this Michelin-listed waterfront restaurant, the scallops with asparagus and smoked Hierro cheese is among the star turns. Great location and good choice of wines.

El Equilibrista 33 €€€ *Calle Ingeniero Salinas 23, tel: 928 234 326, www.restauranteelequilibrista33.es*. Listed in the Michelin Guide, *El Equilibrista* is a warm and welcoming farm-to-table restaurant serving traditional cuisine made from Canarian products. The team gives a surprising twist to recipes, keeping the whole dining experience fun and exciting.

La Marinera €€€ *Alonso Ojeda, Paseo de las Canteras La Puntilla, tel: 928 461 555/928 468 802*, www.restaurantelamarineralaspalmas.com. At the end of Playa de las Canteras, this restaurant has a dining room so close to the sea that you could almost catch the fish yourself. Fortunately, they do it for you, and cook it extremely well. Barbecued meats are also on offer, as are Canarian wines.

Muxgo €€€ *Santa Cataliana, a Royal Hideaway Hotel, C/León y Castillo 227, tel: 606 654 271*, www.muxgo.es. Chef Borja Marrero champions sustainable cuisine at *Muxgo*, prioritizing organic ingredients sourced from his own farm and across the island, and has been awarded a Michelin Green Star for his efforts. Dishes are creative and contemporary, served in a light and airy dining space in *Santa Cataliana, a Royal Hideaway Hotel*.

Poemas €€€€ *Santa Catalina, a Royal Hideaway Hotel, C/León y Castillo 227, tel: 928 243 041*, www.restaurantepoemas.com. Run by the esteemed Padrón brother-chefs, it is unsurprising that *Poemas* has scooped a Michelin star for its culinary credentials. Young chef Icíar Pérez helms the kitchen, giving a creative spin to traditional recipes. Choose between the a la carte and an excellent tasting menu. The dining room is refined and elegant, with acres of gleaming wood accented by jewel-toned velvet chairs and checkerboard flooring.

Ribera del Río Miño €€€ *Calle Olof Palme, 21, Las Palmas de Gran Canaria, tel: 928 264 431*, www.riberadelriomino.com. A pricey but popular restaurant close to Playa de las Canteras and Plaza España. Recommended for its Galician cuisine and good wines.

Tabaiba €€€ *C/Portugal 79, tel: 928 027 055*, www.tabaibarestaurante.com. The brainchild of chef Abraham Ortega, this Michelin-starred gem takes its name from a native flower. Playful, imaginative dishes made from local island produce are served to diners in an intimate dining space; two tasting menus are available.

THE EAST

Agüimes

Restaurant El Guachinche €€ *Calle Doctor Joaquín Artiles, tel: 626 201 872.* Near the historic centre, this is a fabulous place to taste authentic Canarian cuisine – the roasted cheese is very good. Reserve a table on the terrace.

Santa Brígida

Bodegón Vandama €€€ *Carretera Bandama, 116, tel: 928 352 754,* www. bodegonvandama.com. This charming tavern is off the beaten track – and all the better for it. Surrounded by vineyards and gardens, its speciality is the *parrilla* (grilled meats) served with tasty salsas, pimienta or Roquefort.

THE SOUTH

Maspalomas and Meloneras

La Casa Vieja €€ *Calle el Lomo 139, Carretera de Fataga, tel: 928 077 891.* Under new ownership since 2021, this iconic rustic restaurant has been refurbished and is now a perfect mix of traditional and modern decor. The food too is classic with a contemporary spin.

Ceniza Restaurante €€€ *Paseo Boulevard El Faro, tel: 686 874 202,* www.ceniza-restaurante.com. Right on the waterfront promenade, *Ceniza* offers fine dining with a Spanish twist in a chic, contemporary space. The dishes are beautifully presented, and the flavours distinctive. The catch of the day is a popular choice.

La Proa Casa Reyes Meloneras €€ *Centro Comercial Meloneras Playa, Local 103, tel: 928 142 403.* This smart restaurant, with its excellent location and fantastic sea views, is also great value. The fresh fish is the highlight here.

Samsara €€ *Avenida del Oasis 30, Maspalomas, tel: 928 142 736,* www.samsara-gc.com. This Asian-fusion restaurant is an ideal location for a romantic evening; highlights include the tuna and duck *carpaccio*. Advance booking is recommended.

El Senador €€€ *Paseo del Faro 2, tel: 928 142 068*. Located on Maspalomas beach, opposite el Faro, this marine-themed restaurant is a locals' favourite for lunch. It specializes in rice dishes and paellas, fresh fish and grilled meats plus home-made desserts.

Playa del Inglés

360° Restaurant €€€ *Bohemia Suites & Spa, Avenida Estados Unidos 28, tel: 928 563 400*. With panoramic views over Maspalomas Dunes, this glass-fronted restaurant draws on culinary influences around the world without losing the essence of Canarian food. Sharing the space is *Atelier Cocktail bar*, a perfect spot to linger over a drink after dinner.

Las Cumbres €€ *Avenida de Tirajana 11, tel: 928 760 941*. This long-standing favourite is decorated with old agricultural and domestic utensils. It specializes in dishes from various regions of Spain, particularly slow-roasted lamb, splendid Iberian hams, and prawns from Huelva.

Lovin Food €€€ *Avenida de Tirajana 3, tel: 828 991 029*, www.lovinfood.es. Charming hosts Maurizio and Cristina focus on fusion and modern Italian-style cooking at their small restaurant. Each dish is prepared with passion and designed to be shared. There are just seven tables so book ahead.

Taberna La Caña €€ *Avenida Tenerife 4, tel: 928 761 553*, www.tabernalacana. es. A family-friendly restaurant with a children's menu, a few streets back from the beach. Expect reliably good Mediterranean food; the paella is a highlight.

Tenderete del Sabor €€ *Avenida de Tirajana 3, tel: 928 968 762*, www.tenderetedelsabor.eatbu.com. On the ground floor of an apartment block, *Tenderete del Sabor* may not look much from outside, but don't be misled: this unassuming restaurant has served consistently good food for years. A locals' favourite, it specializes in Columbian and local dishes.

Arguineguín

La Aquarela €€€€ *Apartamentos Aquamarina, Playa de Patalavaca*, www. restaurantelaaquarela.com. Helmed by chef Germán Ortega, this Michelin-starred restaurant is one of the hottest names on the island's restaurant scene. Delicate, highly technical dishes are rooted in place but given an occasional playful Nordic twist, inspired by Ortega's time working in Stockholm.

Puerto Rico and Amadores

Beach Restaurant and Lounge at Amadores Beach Club €€ *Playa Amadores, tel: 928 560 056*. You can expect an exceptional attention to detail at this chilled beach club, where a creative seasonal menu offers a fusion of flavours, from boat-fresh sushi to rice dishes and seafood pasta.

KAIA €€€ *Gloria Palace Royal Hotel, Playa Amadores, Calle Tamara 1, tel: 928 128 640*. A glass-fronted restaurant spills outside onto a breeze-cooled terrace, with fine views of Playa de Amadores. The menu is dominated by fresh fish – the sea bass is delicious – along with grilled meats and rice dishes. Staff are warm and welcoming; service is attentive.

Restaurante Que Bien €€ *Calle Tasartico, tel: 928 725 963*. With dim lighting and a warm welcome, *Que Bien* makes you feel right at home – and that's before you sample the exceptional cooking. The chef often comes up with his own creations, such as ravioli with roasted pork ribs sautéed with honey, parmesan cream cheese and toasted almonds. Plus, the bay view is to die for.

Puerto de Mogán and Mogán

Los Guayres €€€ *Hotel Cordial Mogán Playa, Avenida Los Marrero 2, tel: 928 724 100, www.losguayres.com*. Chef Alexis Álvarez heads up the Michelin-starred kitchen, fusing Canarian cuisine with contemporary culinary influences. Fresh fish and seafood takes centre stage on the menu, along with traditional meat dishes such as goat and suckling pig.

La Cofradía €€ *Dársena Exterior s/n, tel: 928 565 321*. A locals' hangout on the fishermen's quay, where that day's catch comes straight off the boats. If you're splashing out, go for the *cazuela de langosta* (lobster casserole).

Patio Canario € *Urbanizacíon Puerto de Mogán, tel: 928 565 456*. Overlooking the harbour, this friendly restaurant serves fresh fish and local specialities, and is a lovely place to sit and watch the boats. Best value is the catch of the day, served grilled and with vegetables.

Acaymo €€ *Calle los Pasitos 21, tel: 928 569 263,* www.restauranteacaymogan. es. This former village school has been reimagined as a rustic restaurant, serving traditional island dishes, fish stews and roast meats.

Casa Enrique €€ *Calle San José 3, tel: 928 569 542.* Big, rather old-fashioned looking place in the main street where the proprietor dishes up local food such as *puchero* and *rancho canario* as well as grilled fish and steaks.

THE WEST AND NORTH

Agaete

La Quisquilla €€€ *Avenida Alfredo Kraus 41, El Turmán, tel: 928 477 696,* www. laquisquilla.com. Set in a fishing village, it's not surprising the seafood at *La Quisquilla* is excellent; the chef often comes out to check everything is in order. Glass and wood give the interior a trendy vibe, and there's a pretty terrace.

Arucas

Casa Brito €€€ *Pasaje Ter 17, tel: 928 622 323,* www.casabrito.com. *Casa Brito* is famed for its perfectly cooked meats and fresh fish prepared in different sauces. Of the two rustic dining rooms, the main one has an open wood grill and wood ceilings. Be sure to taste the home-made guava ice cream.

Puerto de las Nieves

Las Nasas €€ *Calle Nuestra Señora de las Nieves 6, tel: 928 898 650.* One of a row of fish restaurants overlooking the port, *Las Nasas* has a cavernous dining room opening out onto an outdoor terrace. Try the signature *ropa vieja* with octopus (*pulpo*). Popular with Las Palmas de Gran Canaria weekenders.

Ragú €€ *Paseo de los Poetas 10, Puerto de las Nieves, tel: 928 886 425,* www. ragu.rest. One of the best seafood restaurants in this little port. On the menu, you'll find octopus salad, fresh fish and shrimps.

Teror

Como Como 15 €€ *Los Viñatigos 15, tel: 639 844 463*. Tucked away from the tourist area, this cosy little restaurant offers a short menu of authentic local dishes cooked to a high standard. The relaxed dining room has a great vibe.

THE CENTRE

Artenara

Mirador La Cilla € *Camino la Cilla 9, tel: 609 163 944*. This is the famous cave restaurant, with spectacular views from its sun-bleached terrace, and kitchens cut into the rock. It serves typical, robust meat dishes, many doused in *mojo* sauce.

San Mateo

Casa Martell €€ *Carretera Centro, Madronal, tel: 928 641 283*, www.casamartell. es. In a lovely spot halfway between San Mateo and Santa Brigida, this restaurant can't be missed thanks to its mural-painted facade. Host Antonio is very welcoming and serves up Canarian cuisine that respects island traditions.

Santa Lucía

El Mirador de Santa Lucia €€€ *Calle Maestro Enrique Hernández, n 5, tel: 928 798 005*. This spacious restaurant serves up hearty local dishes like *salpicón de marisco o garbanzada* (seafood with onions, garlic, tomatoes and peppers) but the biggest draw here is the terrace view of the *barranco* (ravine).

Tejeda

Asador Grill Yolanda €€ *Cruz de Tejeda, tel: 928 666 276*, www.asadoryolanda. com. Good-value *asados* (roast meats) washed down with Canarian wines served on a covered terrace with views of Tenerife's El Teide on a clear day.

Parador Cruz de Tejeda €€ *Cruz de Tejeda, tel: 928 012 500*. At a lofty 1560m, this cloud-raking restaurant serves up fine views alongside its sophisticated Canarian cuisine.

TRAVEL ESSENTIALS

PRACTICAL INFORMATION

A

ACCESSIBLE TRAVEL

Gando airport and most modern hotels have wheelchair access and facilities for travellers with disabilities, as do the newer museums. For general information, consult the *Able Magazine* (Pentagon Centre, 36–38 Washington Street, Glasgow G3 8AZ, tel: 0141 285 4000, www.ablemagazine.co.uk). Tourism for All (tel: 0845 124 9971, www.tourismforall.org.uk) also provides information for travellers with disabilities. Check the Canary government site www.gran-canariaaccesible.info for the most up-to-date information.

ACCOMMODATION

Accommodation on Gran Canaria is concentrated mainly in Las Palmas de Gran Canaria and in large, modern hotels apartment complexes in the southern resorts. Elsewhere, there is not a great deal of choice. You will not find much budget accommodation in the resorts. In Puerto Rico, there are mostly self-catering apartments and 'aparthotels'.

Hotels are rated by the Canarian government from one to five stars. Ratings depend largely on facilities; prices within the categories may vary considerably. Breakfast is usually included in the basic rate in resort hotels and larger establishments. Package holidays are most economical, offering accommodation in large, comfortable hotels, usually with pools, and in self-catering apartments. Even if you don't want to spend your holiday in the resorts, they can provide a convenient base. Many hotels have adults-only and/or minimum-stay policies.

There are also apartments and 'aparthotels', where each room has kitchen facilities yet retains all the trappings of a hotel. Apartments are graded with one to four 'keys' depending on amenities. It is wise to book accommodation in advance, especially during the two high seasons – November to April and July to August.

In the interior there is a number of *casas rurales* – rural properties or old townhouses that have been converted into small, medium-priced hotels or renovated and rented as self-catering accommodation. Contact Gran Canaria Rural (Calle Tenerife 24, Las Palmas de Gran Canaria, tel: 928 464 464, www. grancanariarural.com).

I would like a single/ double room **Quisiera una habitación sencilla/doble**
With/without bathroom and toilet/shower **con/sin baño/ ducha**
What's the rate per night? **¿Cuál es el precio por noche?**
Is breakfast included? **¿Está incluído el desayuno?**

AIRPORT

Gando airport is on the east coast, about 20km (12 miles) south of Las Palmas de Gran Canaria. Bus No. 60 goes to Las Palmas de Gran Canaria (Parque San Telmo and Parque Santa Catalina terminals) at 15 and 45 minutes past the hour (6.15am–11.15pm). The journey takes about 30 minutes and currently costs €2.30 (San Telmo) and €2.95 (Santa Catalina). There is also an hourly bus (No. 66) to Maspalomas between 7.20am and 8.20pm (journey time 30–40 minutes, cost €4.05), although most visitors going to the resorts will be on package holidays and will be collected at the airport by their tour operator. A taxi from the airport to Las Palmas de Gran Canaria centre costs about approximately €30.

Gando airport: tel: 913 211 000 (24 hours), www.aena.es.

B

BICYCLE HIRE

Bikes can be hired in the resorts. For top-notch mountain and road bikes, try Free Motion, *Sandy Beach Hotel,* Avenida Alferéces Provisionales 6–8, Playa del Inglés, tel: 928 777 479, www.free-motion.com; it has outlets across the island so check the website for the most convenient.

BUDGETING FOR YOUR TRIP

Gran Canaria is relatively inexpensive compared with many European destinations. To give you an idea of what to expect, here's a list of some average prices in euros.

Accommodation. Rates for two sharing a double room can range from as low as €60 at a *pensión* or *hostal* to as much as €1000 at a top-end five-star hotel. A pleasant three-star hotel will cost in the range of €120–140. Rates drop considerably out of season – May to June and September to October are the least expensive, and are very pleasant months to be there.

Attractions. Most museums charge a small entry fee of around €4–5. More expensive are the larger attractions such as Palmitos Park (€32 adults, €23 children); Aqualand (€34 adults, €25 children; both venues are cheaper if you buy online); and Cocodrilo Park (€9.90 adults, €6.90 children).

Buses. Single trips in Las Palmas de Gran Canaria, €1.40. Buying a rechargeable *BonoGuagua* Sin Contacto cuts the price by about a third. Bus from Playa del Inglés to Las Palmas de Gran Canaria, about €8 return.

Car hire. Including comprehensive insurance and tax, rates are around €40 a day from the big international companies; you get a better deal if you book for a week. Cars booked in advance online may be considerably cheaper (see Car Hire).

Getting there. Air fares vary enormously; those from the UK range between £160 and £600 (€210–790). You get the best deals May–June and Sept–Oct. From the US, flights cost around $1,000 (€1000). Cheapest flights are usually available online.

Meals and drinks. In a bar, a continental breakfast (fresh orange juice, coffee and toast or croissant) will cost around €5. The cheapest three-course set meal – the *menú del día* – including one drink, will be €8–10. The average price of a three-course à la carte meal, including house wine, will be about €25 per person. At the top restaurants, you may pay double that.

Petrol. Though prices fluctuate, petrol is around €1.20 a litre.

Taxis. Prices are controlled, and reasonable. From the airport to Las Palmas de Gran Canaria, the fare is around €30. Most trips within the city, and around Playa del Inglés, don't cost more than €7.

C

CAMPING

There are a number of free government-run campsites, called *zonas de acampada*, on the island, usually in attractive and sometimes remote places. You must get a permit from OIAC, Calle Bravo Murillo Las Palmas de Gran Canaria, tel: 928 219 229, www.cabildo.grancanaria.com.

CAR HIRE (see also Driving)

You must be over 21, sometimes 24, to hire a car, and to have held a licence for at least 24 months. You need your passport and a credit card. There are dozens of local companies, especially in Playa del Inglés, and these tend to be cheaper. It is also cheaper to hire a car online; **CICAR** (Canary Islands Car), tel: 928 822 900, www.cicar.com, has been operating for over 30 years. Autos Moreno is a tried and tested local company (tel: 928 268 314, www.autos-moreno.es). All the big international companies have offices at the airport, in Las Palmas de Gran Canaria and in the resorts.

Airport offices: Avis tel 928 092 330, www.avis.es; Europcar tel: 911 505 000, www.europcar.es; Budget tel: 928 092 330, www.budget.es.

I'd like to rent a car for one day/week. **Quisiera alquilar un coche por un día/una semana.**
Please include full insurance. **Haga el favor de incluir el seguro a todo riesgo.**

CLIMATE

In the south, sunshine is practically guaranteed all year round. Winter temperatures average 22–24°C (72–75°F), summer averages are 26–28°C (79–82°F), although they often exceed 30°C (86°F). It can be very windy, even in the hottest months. In the north of the island, temperatures are a few degrees lower and there is more cloud. Higher regions of the mountainous interior, of course, are much cooler. Some rain falls from Nov–Jan and in April, but showers are usually short.

CLOTHING

Light summer clothes, sandals and a swimsuit are all you need for much of the time, but bring a sweater or jacket for cooler evenings and for trips to the mountains, and strong shoes if you want to do any walking. A jacket and tie for men and a smart dress for women is appreciated, but not obligatory, in more expensive restaurants. Don't offend local sensibilities by wearing swimwear or skimpy clothing in city streets, museums or churches.

CRIME AND SAFETY

Crime rates are not high, but there is quite a lot of opportunistic bag-snatching and pick-pocketing in tourist areas, especially at markets or fiestas. Robberies from cars are most prevalent, so never leave anything of value in a car. If you have one, use the safe deposit box in your room for valuables, including your passport (carrying a photocopy of your passport is a good idea). Burglaries of holiday apartments occur, too, so keep doors and windows locked when you are out. Report all thefts to the police within 24 hours for your own insurance purposes.

I want to report a theft. **Quiero denunciar un robo.**

D

DRIVING

Driving conditions. The rules are the same as in continental Europe: drive on the right, pass on the left, yield right of way to vehicles coming from your right. Coastal and mountain roads can be extremely sinuous and full of hairpin bends. In rural areas, you may meet a herd of goats, a donkey cart, a large pothole or falling rocks.

Speed limits. 120 km/h (74 mph) on motorways, 100 km/h (62 mph) on dual carriageways, 90 km/h (52mph) on country roads, 50 km/h (31 mph) in built-up areas and 20 km/h (13mph) in residential areas.

Motorways. Toll-free.

Traffic and parking. In most towns, traffic can be heavy, one-way systems confusing, and road signs inadequate. Early afternoon is a good time to get in and out of towns, and to find a parking space. It is an offence to park facing the traffic. Don't park on white or yellow lines. Blue lines indicate pay-and-display parking areas.

Petrol. Petrol is much cheaper than in the UK and the rest of Europe, but prices have risen. Unleaded petrol is *sin plomo*. Some larger petrol stations are open 24 hours, and most accept credit cards. In the mountainous centre, there are very few petrol stations.

Aparcamiento Parking
Desviación Detour
Obras Road works
Peatones Pedestrians
Peligro Danger
Salida de camiones Truck exit
Senso único One way
¿Se puede aparcar aqui? Can I park here?
Llénelo, por favor. Fill the tank please.
Ha habido un accidente. There has been an accident.

Rules and regulations. Always carry your driving licence with you. It is a good idea to have a photocopy of your passport. Seat belts are compulsory. Children under 10 must travel in the rear. Using mobile phones or GPS devices while driving is illegal.

Traffic police. Armed civil guards (Guardia Civil) patrol the roads on motor-cycles. In towns, municipal police handle traffic control. If you are fined for a traffic offence, you may have to pay on the spot.

E

ELECTRICITY

220 volts is standard, with continental-style two-pin sockets. Adapters are available in UK shops and at airports. American 110V appliances need a trans-former.

EMBASSIES AND CONSULATES

UK: Calle Luís Morote 6, Las Palmas de Gran Canaria, tel: 928 262 508.
US: Calle Martínez Escobar 3, Oficina 7, Las Palmas de Gran Canaria, tel: 928 222 552.
Ireland: Calle León y Castillo 195, Las Palmas de Gran Canaria, tel: 928 297 728.
South Africa: Calle Albareda 54, Las Palmas de Gran Canaria, tel: 928 224 975.

If you lose your passport or run into trouble with the authorities or the police, contact your consulate for advice.

Where is the American/British consulate? **¿Dónde está el consulado americano/británico?**

EMERGENCIES (see also Embassies, Health and Police)

General emergencies: 112
National Police: 091
Local Police: 092
Guardia Civil: 062
Ambulance: 112
Fire Brigade: 112

Police! **Policía!**
Help! **Socorro!**
Fire! **Fuego!**
Stop! **Deténgase!**

G

GETTING THERE

By air. There are numerous direct budget airline flights from all UK airports to Gran Canaria. The flight time is 4–4.5 hours. Iberia, the Spanish national carrier (tel: 020 3684 3774, www.iberia.com), now merged with British Airways (www.britishairways.com), fly via Madrid, which obviously takes longer. Check the web and advertisements in Sunday papers for good flight-only deals, but all-in package holidays can be the cheapest way to go.

At present, there are several flights from the US (including New York, Los Angeles, Chicago) operated by British Airways, Iberia and Lufthansa (www.lufthansa.com). Some flights go via Madrid or Barcelona, or via London airports; check with a travel agency, or visit www.opodo.com. Ryanair (www.ryanair.com), easyJet (www.easyjet.com), Tui (www.tui.co.uk) and Jet2 (www.jet2.com) operate regular flights from London and other British airports.

Inter-island flights are operated by Binter Airlines (tel: 928 327 700, www2.bintercanarias.com).

By ship. Trasmediterránea runs a weekly service from Cádiz to Las Palmas de Gran Canaria, which takes at least two days, and also operates services from Tenerife, Fuerteventura and Lanzarote to Las Palmas de Gran Canaria. For details, tel: 902 454 645 or visit www.trasmediterranea.es.

The Fred Olsen Shipping Line (tel: 928 290 070, www.fredolsen.es) runs ferries from Gran Canaria to Tenerife six times a day from Puerto de las Nieves (near Agaete) (journey time about 70 minutes; free bus from Parque Santa Catalina in Las Palmas de Gran Canaria). Naviera Armas (tel: 902 456 500, www.navieraarmas.com) also has regular services to Tenerife, Fuerteventura and Lanzarote. The crossing to Tenerife takes about 2.5 hours.

H

HEALTH AND MEDICAL CARE

Non-EU visitors should always have private medical insurance, and although there are reciprocal arrangements between EU countries, it is advisable for people from member nations to do the same, because not all eventualities are covered. The GHIC card, which entitles UK citizens to free healthcare, is available online at www.gov.uk/global-health-insurance-card. Before being treated, it is essential to establish that the doctor or service is working within the Spanish Health Service, otherwise you will be sent elsewhere.

Dental treatment is not available under this reciprocal system. Hotel receptionists or private clinics will recommend dentists.

There are two main hospitals in Las Palmas de Gran Canaria: **Hospital Insular** (Plaza Dr Pasteur, Avenida Marítima del Sur, tel: 928 444 000) and **Hospital Dr Negrin** (Barranco de la Ballena, just off the GC-23 to the south of the city, tel: 928 450 000). The **Red Cross** (Cruz Roja) is based at Calle León y Castillo 231, Las Palmas de Gran Canaria, tel: 928 290 000. Private hospitals include the **San Roque University Hospitals** – one at Calle Dolores de la Rocha 5, Las Palmas de Gran Canaria, tel: 928 404 040; the other Calle Mar de Siberia 1, Maspalomas, tel: 928 063 615 – and **San José Hospital** on Las Canteras Beach (Calle Padre Cueto 26, tel: 928 263 708).

In the resorts, there are numerous private clinics where you will have to pay for treatment on the spot and reclaim it on your medical insurance. The Las Palmeras chain has clinics in Maspalomas, Playa del Inglés and San Agustín, tel: 928 763 366, www.clinicalaspalmeras.com. In Puerto Rico, the British Medical Clinic (Avenida Tomás Roca Bosch 4, tel: 928 560 016) is reliable. In an emergency, call 112 for an ambulance.

Most problems visitors experience are due to too much sun, too much alcohol or food that they are unused to – problems that can often be dealt with by **farmácias** (chemists/drugstores). Spanish pharmacists are highly trained and can often dispense medicines over the counter that would need a prescription in the UK. They are open during shopping hours; after hours, one in each town remains open all night, the *farmácia de guardia*, and its location is posted in the window of all other *farmácias* and in local newspapers.

Where's the nearest (all-night) chemist? **¿Dónde está la farmácia (de guardia) más cercana?**
I need a doctor/dentist **Necesito un médico/dentista**
sunburn/sunstroke **quemadura del sol/una insolación**
an upset stomach **molestias de estómago**
Is this service public or private? **¿Es este servicio público o privado?**

I

INTERNET

Most hotels, cafés, bars and restaurants across the island offer good internet connections, and many public spaces offer free wi-fi, such as parks, beaches and public transport. In the resorts, you will find wi-fi with no trouble. In terms of consistency, mobile connection is most troublesome in the south around Mogan, Playa de Tauro and Taurito, due to the territory morphology.

L

LANGUAGE

The Spanish spoken in the Canary Islands is slightly different from that of the mainland. For instance, islanders don't lisp when they pronounce the letters c or z. A number of Latin American words and expressions are used. The most common are *guagua* (pronounced *wah-wah*), meaning bus, and *papa* (potato). In tourist areas basic English, German and some French is spoken, or at least understood.

The *Rough Guide Spanish Phrasebook and Dictionary* covers most of the situations you may encounter in Spain and the Canary Islands.

Do you speak English? **¿Habla usted inglés?**
I don't speak Spanish. **No hablo español.**

LGBTQ+ TRAVEL

Gran Canaria is a very LGBTQ-friendly destination, with the main gay scene in Maspalomas. The Yumbo Centre is at the heart of the action, with plenty of queer bars, clubs, open-air terraces and drag shows. Popular events on the LGBTQ+ calendar include the Freedom Festival, Maspalomas Pride and the Maspalomas Carnival (and its world-famous Drag Queen Gala in particular). Visit www.gaymaspalomas.com for more information.

M

MAPS

Most tourist offices will give you free maps, which should be sufficient. For something more detailed, go to the official government bookshop, Librería del Cabildo Insular, Calle Cano 24, Las Palmas de Gran Canaria, tel: 928 381 539, www.libroscanarios.org. Be aware that many road numbers have changed and the ones on the new maps don't always match those on the road signs.

Do you have a map of the city/island? **¿Tiene un plano de la a ciudad/isla?**

MEDIA

Radio and television. Many hotels have satellite tv with several stations in various languages, including CNN. RTVC is a local station, which includes some English language news and tourist information in its programming. English-language radio stations include Kiss FM Live 102.5 MHz, Power FM 98.2 MHz and UK Away FM 99.9 MHz.

Newspapers and periodicals. Major British and Continental newspapers are on sale in the resorts and Las Palmas de Gran Canaria on the day of publication. A number of English-language publications have island news and tourist information but are not evenly distributed.

For Spanish speakers, the island newspapers are *Canarias7* and *La Provincia: Diario de Las Palmas*. Both of these contain listings of events so they can be useful, even if your Spanish is very sketchy. *El País* and other Spanish national newspapers are also available.

MONEY

Currency. The monetary unit in the Canary Islands, as throughout Spain, is the euro, abbreviated €.

Bank notes are available in denominations of €500, 200, 100, 50, 20, 10 and 5. The euro is subdivided into 100 cents and there are coins available for €1 and €2 and for 50, 20, 10, 5, 2 and 1 cent.

Currency exchange. Banks are the preferred place to exchange currency but *casas de cambio* also change money, as do some travel agencies, and these stay open outside banking hours. The larger hotels may also change guests' money, at a slightly less advantageous rate. Always take your passport when you go to change money.

Credit cards. Major international cards are widely recognized, although smaller businesses might prefer cash. Visa/Eurocard/MasterCard are most generally accepted. Credit and debit cards, with a PIN number, are also useful for obtaining euros from ATMs – cash machines – which are to be found in all towns and resorts. They offer the most convenient way of obtaining cash and will usually give you the best exchange rate.

Where's the nearest bank/currency exchange office? **¿Dónde está el banco más cercano/la oficina de cambio más cercana?**

I want to change some dollars/pounds. **Quiero cambiar dólares/libres esterlina.**

Do you accept traveller's cheques? **¿Acepta usted cheques de viajero?**

Can I pay with this credit card? **¿Puedo pagar con esta tarjeta de crédito?**

O

OPENING TIMES

Shops and offices are usually open Monday to Saturday 10am–1.30pm and 5–8.30pm (although some close on Saturday afternoon). Large supermarkets may stay open all day, as do many shops in the tourist resorts, and some also open on Sunday. Banks usually open Monday to Friday 8.30am–2pm; post offices Monday to Saturday 8.30am–2pm.

P

POLICE

There are three police forces in Gran Canaria, as in the rest of Spain. The green-uniformed Guardia Civil (Civil Guard) is the main force. Each town also has its own Policía Municipal (municipal or local police), whose uniform can vary but is mostly blue and black. The third force, the Cuerpo Nacional de Policía is a national anti-crime unit that sports a dark blue uniform. All police officers are armed. Spanish police are strict, but courteous to foreign visitors.

National Police: 091
Local Police: 092
Guardia Civil: 062

Where is the nearest police station? **¿Dónde está la comisaría más cercana?**

POST OFFICES

Post offices (www.correos.es) are for mail and telegrams, not telephone calls. The main post office in Las Palmas de Gran Canaria is at Avenida Primero de Mayo 62; in Playa del Inglés, it is at Edificio Mercurio, Avenida de Tirajana. Stamps *(sellos)* are also sold at tobacconist's *(estanco)* and by most shops selling postcards. Mailboxes are painted yellow. The slot marked *extranjero* is for letters abroad.

Where is the (nearest) post office? **¿Dónde está la oficina de correos (más cercana)?**
A stamp for this letter/postcard, please. **Por favor, un sello para esta carta/tarjeta.**

PUBLIC HOLIDAYS

1 January *Año Nuevo* New Year's Day
6 January *Epifanía* Epiphany
1 May *Día del Trabajo* Labour Day
30 May *Día de las Islas Canarias* Canary Islands' Day
May/June *Corpus Christi* Corpus Christi
25 July *Santiago Apóstol* St James' Day
15 August *Asunción* Assumption
12 October *Día de la Hispanidad* Columbus Day
1 November *Todos los Santos* All Saints' Day
6 December *Dia de la Constitución* Constitution Day
8 December *Inmaculada Concepción* Immaculate Conception
25/26 December *Navidad* Christmas Day

Movable dates:

Carnaval week of Shrove Tuesday/February or early March, depending on the date of Easter

Jueves Santo Maundy Thursday

Viernes Santo Good Friday

In addition to these, each municipality decides two of its own, one of which is normally its patron saint's day.

R

RELIGION

The majority religion is Roman Catholic; church attendance is quite high. Respect people's privacy when visiting churches. There are also Anglican, Muslim, Jewish, Mormon and other religious communities.

T

TAXES

The Impuesto Generalisado Indirecto Canario (IGIC) is levied on all bills at a rate of 7 percent. The tax is not usually included in the price you are quoted for hotel rooms.

TELEPHONES

Calling directly from your hotel room is expensive unless you are using a card from a local long-distance supplier such as at&t or mci. Get the free connection number applicable to Spain from the supplier before you leave (they are different for each country).

For international calls, wait for the dial tone, then dial 00, wait for a second tone and dial the country code, area code (minus any initial zero) and the number. Country codes are: UK: 44, Ireland: 353, US and Canada: 1, Australia: 61, New Zealand: 64.

International Operator: 025.

Telephone codes for the Canary Islands (which must always be dialled as part of the number, even for local calls): Gran Canaria, Lanzarote and Fuerteventura: 928; Tenerife, El Hierro, La Gomera and La Palma: 922.

TIME ZONES

The time in the Canaries is the same as in the UK, Greenwich Mean Time, but 1 hour behind the rest of Europe, including Spain, and 5 hours ahead of New York. Like the rest of Europe, the islands adopt summer time (putting the clocks forward by an hour) from the end of March through to the end of September.

TIPPING

A service charge is often included in restaurant bills (look for the words *servicio incluído*), so an extra tip is not expected. If it is not included, add around 10 percent, which is also the usual tip for taxi drivers and hairdressers. In bars, customers usually leave a few coins, rounding up the bill. A hotel porter will appreciate €1 for carrying bags to your room; tip hotel maids according to your length of stay.

TOILETS

Toilets in the Canaries are usually called *servicios* or *aseos*. Public conveniences can be found in beach areas and bus stations, and are, for the most part, well-maintained. If using lavatories belonging to bars or restaurants, it is considered polite to buy at least a coffee. Some don't ask questions of casual visitors; other proprietors keep the key behind the bar to make sure their toilets are not used by the general public.

Where are the lavatories? **¿Dónde están los servicios?**

TOURIST INFORMATION
Tourist offices abroad
Canada: 2 Bloor Street West, Suite 3402, Toronto, Ontario M4W 3E2, tel: 1-416-961 3131.

Ireland: Callaghan House, 13–16 Dame Street, Dublin 2, tel: 01-6350 200.

UK: 2nd Floor Heron House, 10 Dean Farrar Street, London SW1H 0DX, tel: 020 7317 2011 (no personal callers at office).

US: 60 East 42nd Street, Suite 5300 (53rd Floor), New York, NY 10165-0039, tel: 212 265 8822.

See www.spain.info/en/query/spanish-tourist-offices-abroad for a full list of Spanish tourist offices abroad.

Tourist offices in Gran Canaria

Most towns have a tourist office, open during normal business hours. Some of the main ones are:

Las Palmas de Gran Canaria: Oficina de Turismo de Gran Canaria, Calle Triana 93, tel: 928 219 600, www.grancanaria.com.

Agaete: Calle Nuestra Señora de las Nieves 1, tel: 928 554 382, www.agaete.es.

Agüimes: Plaza de San Antón s/n, tel: 928 789 980, www.visitaguimes.com.

Arucas: Calle León y Castillo 10, tel: 928 623 136, www.turismoarucas.com.

Gáldar: Calle Plaza de Santiago 1, tel: 928 880 050, www.tourismo.galdar.es.

Maspalomas/Playa de Inglés: Calla Les Dunas 2, tel: 928 723 400, www.turismo.maspalomas.com.

Paseo Marítimo, Centro Comercial Anexo II, tel: 928 768 409.

Puerto de Mogán/Puerto Rico: Avenida de Mogán 1, tel: 928 158 804, www.mogan.es.

San Agustín: Centro Comercial El Portón, tel: 928 769 262, www.turismo.maspalomas.com.

Tejeda: Calle Leocadio Cabrera s/n, tel: 928 666 189, www.tejeda.es.

TRANSPORT

There is no train service, but the bus service is cheap and reliable. In Las Palmas de Gran Canaria, there are two subterranean terminals, in Parque San Telmo and adjacent to Parque Santa Catalina. Tickets on the *guaguas* (buses) cost €1.40. A rechargeable card *BonoGuagua* Sin Contacto (pronounced *bono wawa*) is good value (€8.50) and can be bought in the terminals and in kiosks. City buses run from dawn until 9.30pm, and there's a night service on major routes (tel: 928 305 800, www.guaguas.com).

Long-distance buses leave either from the Parque San Telmo bus station or the Parque Santa Catalina terminal. Buses to the southern resorts are frequent and leave as soon as they are full. They are run by the Global company, which has a centralized information number: tel: 928 252 630, www.guaguasglobal.com. In Playa del Inglés and Maspalomas, services are efficient and run to all the main out-of-town attractions. (For inter-island ferries and flights, see Getting There.)

Taxis. The letters sp (*servicio público*) on the front and rear bumpers of a car indicate that it is a taxi. It may also have a green light in the front windscreen or a green sign indicating '*libre*' when it is free. There is no shortage of taxis in urban areas, and there are usually taxi ranks in the main squares. In towns, the fare is calculated by a meter; for longer, out-of-town journeys there are fixed tariffs, but you may feel happier if you agree an approximate fare in advance. Taxis are good value, with the longest run in Las Palmas de Gran Canaria costing around €7; from the airport, the fare is around €30. In the southern resorts, where taxis belong to a local co-operative (tel: 928 154 777, www.taxismaspalomas.es), it is also a good, inexpensive way to travel.

V

VISAS AND ENTRY REQUIREMENTS

Most visitors, including citizens of all EU countries, the UK, US, Canada, Ireland, Australia and New Zealand, only need a valid passport. No inoculations are required. Although the islands are part of the EU, there is a restriction on duty-free goods that can be brought back to the UK. The allowance is 200 cigarettes, or 50 cigars or 250g tobacco; 1 litre spirits over 22 percent, or 2 litres under 22 percent and 4 litres of wine.

W

WATER

The island suffers from a water shortage, so try not to waste it. It is best to avoid drinking tap water. Bottled water is available everywhere and is inexpensive. *Con gas* is sparkling, *sin gas* is still. Firgas water, produced in the north of the island, is the nicest.

WEBSITES

You can find a lot of useful information online before you start your holiday. Some helpful sites are:

www.grancanaria.com Oficial de Turismo de Gran Canaria site.

www.spain.info A branch of the official tourist office site.

www.spain-grancanaria.com An excellent general site.

www.hellocanaryislands.com General information site with hotel listings.

www.grancanarianaturalandactive.com For nature, rural and active holidays in Gran Canaria.

www.grancanariablue.com The best nautical experiences in Gran Canaria.

www.grancanariawellness.com Spa, wellness and health.

www.grancanariatribikerun.com Cycling and running adventures.

www.grancanariagolf.com Golf in Gran Canaria.

WHERE TO STAY

Gran Canaria has a wide range of accommodation to cater to all tastes and budgets. Tourist-focused beach resorts are located mainly in the south of the island, and range from luxury five-stars with swimming pools, high-end restaurants and extensive spa and wellness facilities, through to wallet-friendly no-frills options. Whatever your budget, there's an abundance of hotels, apartments, bungalows and villas across the island to pick from.

Las Palmas de Gran Canaria has a scattering of lovely boutique bolt-holes in the old quarter, plus urban beach hotels, apartments and *vivienda vacacional* clustered around Playa de las Canteras. In the centre of the island and to the north, you'll find traditional rural hotels, back-to-nature escapes and even cave accommodation.

Prices given are for two people sharing a double room in high season. Breakfast is usually included in hotels in the top three brackets; tax (IGIC) at 7 percent is extra (prices are an approximate guide only).

€€€€ **over 226 euros**
€€€ **126–225 euros**
€€ **76–125 euros**
€ **under 75 euros**

LAS PALMAS DE GRAN CANARIA

AC-Gran Canaria €€€ *Calle Eduardo Benot 3-5, tel: 928 266 100*, http://achotels.marriott.com. This 25-storey hotel, close to Parque Santa Catalina, has 227 functional rooms. Ask for one on an upper floor: you get a great view, the rooftop pool and restaurant are closer, and the traffic noise is less disturbing. Geared more towards business travellers and those on short city breaks.

Bex Hotel €€€ *Calle León & Castillo 330, tel: 928 971 071,* www.designplus-hotels.com. Boutique hotel in the heart of Las Palmas de Gran Canaria, with Art Deco-style interiors and an excellent restaurant. The main calling card, though, is the rooftop bar, where you can sip on a cocktail while taking in sweeping views of Las Palmas de Gran Canaria.

Boutique Hotel Cordial Malteses €€€ *Dr Rafael González 3, tel: 928 402 575,* www.becordial.com. This whitewashed Modernist manor house has been reimagined as a charming hotel, with 27 tastefully restored rooms and a rooftop restaurant. Excellent central location in the historic quarter of Las Palmas de Gran Canaria, close to Vegueta; three more boutique properties by Cordial are dotted throughout the capital.

Hotel Cristina by Tigotan €€€ *Calle Gomera 6, tel: 203 608 7631,* www.dream placehotels.com/en/hotel-cristina. Right on the beach, the largest hotel in town has all the extras expected of a five-star, including a large swimming pool, cocktail bar, restaurants and parking. Definitely not a place for those looking for a calm and relaxing break.

Reina Isabel €€€ *Calle Alfredo L. Jones 40, tel: 928 260 100,* www.bullhotels. com. Smartly renovated, and with an excellent location on Playa de las Canteras, the *Reina Isabel* is a comfortable and reliably good place to stay. There is a rooftop swimming pool and a gym, and the *Summum* restaurant is widely recommended.

Santa Catalina, a Royal Hideaway Hotel by Barceló €€€€ *Parque Doramas, Calle León y Castillo 227, tel: 928 243 040,* www.barcelo.com. Set in a lush park and founded in 1890, this is the oldest, grandest and most exclusive hotel in town. Rooms are scattered with antiques; there's a rooftop bar, a spa and a string of excellent restaurants. Staying here is an unforgettable experience.

THE SOUTH

Maspalomas and Meloneras

H10 Playa Meloneras Palace €€€ *Mar Caspio 5, tel: 928 128 282,* www.h10 hotels.com. Facing the sea, this cliffside hotel brushes up against the fairways of an exclusive golf course. Saying that, you'd be hard-pressed to drag yourself away from the resort's swimming pools, Despacio Spa and half-dozen bars and restaurants.

Hotel Faro, A Lopesan Collection €€€€ *Plaza de Colón, tel: 928 142 214,* www.lopesan.com. Perched on the Faro Boulevard, this sleek hotel overlooks the Atlantic Ocean and Maspalomas Lighthouse. An infinity pool frames blue-on-blue views while the Sky Lounge rooftop bar is the place to go for cocktails and live music.

Hotel Riu Gran Canaria €€€ *Mar mediterráneo s/n, tel: 871 966 296,* www.riu. com. With family rooms and romantic swim-up suites, adults-only pools and kids' splash parks with slides, this all-inclusive hotel manages to successfully cater to both couples and guests with children alike.

Lopesan Baobab Resort €€€€ *Calle Mar Adriático 1, tel: 928 154 400,* www. lopesan.com. With adobe-style buildings and huge baobab sculptures, this striking hotel is designed to resemble an African lodge. A family-friendly resort with plenty of activities to keep kids entertained.

Lopesan Costa Meloneras Resort & Spa €€€€ *Calle Mar Mediterráneo 1, tel: 928 128 100,* www.lopesan.com. This five-star behemoth peeks out from a lush tropical grove, planted with hundreds of palm trees and plants. A huge infinity pool is the jewel in the hotel's crown, though the 3500-square-metre spa with a hydrothermal water circuit might be enough to entice you away.

Lopesan Villa del Conde Resort & Thalasso €€€€ *Calle Mar Mediterráneo 7, tel: 928 563 200,* www.lopesan.com. A picturesque huddle of pastel-painted villas, punctuated with balconies and opening onto courtyards, is rooted in the design of a typical Canarian village. The vibe is warm and welcoming, the service attentive.

Riu Palace Meloneras €€€€ *Mar Mediterráneo s/n, tel: 928 143 182,* www. riu.com. Located in the exclusive enclave of Meloneras, Riu Palace's flagship hotel has bold, eye-popping interiors, five swimming pools set in palm gardens, and a handful of bars and restaurants.

Riu Palace Oasis €€€€ *Plaza de las Palmeras 2, tel: 928 769 500,* www.riu.com. This hotel is set in a palm grove just steps from the dunes, with serene gardens and a lounger-flanked swimming pool. Three restaurants offer a mix of Spanish specialities and fusion cuisine.

Salobre Golf Resort and Serenity €€€ *Calle Swing s/n, tel: 928 943 000,* www.salobrehotel.com. Located on Salobre Golf Resort, with two stunning golf courses for guests to pick from, this peaceful haven is just ten minutes from Meloneras. Not just for golfers, the hotel has an excellent food and wellness offering, too.

Seaside Grand Hotel Residencia €€€€ *Avenida del Oasis 32, tel: 928 723 100;* www.grand-hotel-residencia.com. A member of the Leading Hotels of the World, this multi-award-winning boutique bolthole is among the most exclusive on the island. Traditional-style villas and suites are scattered around a swimming pool amid tropical gardens, tucked away in a palm grove two hundred metres from the dunes. Michelin-starred chef Wolfgang Grobauer takes the helm in the restaurant, and it is surely only a matter of time before he scoops another star for his culinary credentials here.

Seaside Palm Beach €€€€ *Avenida del Oasis, tel: 928 721 032,* www.hotel-palm-beach.com. A member of the Design Hotels group, thanks to its bold 1970s pop art style, and set in lush palm gardens just metres from the beach. There's a clutch of gastronomic restaurants and bars as well as a tranquil spa and a selection of outdoor swimming pools.

Playa del Inglés

Abora Buenaventura by Lopesan €€€ *Calle Gánigo 6, tel: 928 761 650,* www.lopesan.com. Ten minutes' walk from the centre, but there's a free shuttle bus to the beach. However, you barely need to leave what with two swimming pools, three restaurants serving a wide variety of food, entertainment including karaoke, a gym, three tennis courts and a wealth of sports activities.

Abora Continental by Lopesan €€ *Avenida de Italia 2, tel: 928 760 033,* www.lopesan.com. Popular with families thanks to a 'mini' kids' club during school holidays, this all-inclusive hotel also caters to adults with a swimming pool, sauna, solarium and massage treatments, all in lush gardens. There's a volleyball/basketball court and disco.

Barceló Margarita €€€ *Avenida Gran Canaria 38, tel: 928 761 112,* www.barcelo.com. Expect contemporary-style rooms, a brand-new restaurant and an easygoing vibe at this laidback hotel. DJs spin chillout tracks by one of the three outdoor pools, while a kids' club keeps young ones entertained. A free shuttle whisks guests to the beach.

Bohemia Suites & Spa €€€€ *Avenida Estados Unidos 28, tel: 928 563 400;* www.bohemia-grancanaria.com. Located in the centre of Playa del Inglés but only a short hop from the beach, this luxurious adults-only boutique gem is one of only two Design Hotels on the island. Excellent guest facilities include a relaxing spa and wellness area, a beautiful pool set in tropical gardens, a top-floor lounge, and an esteemed restaurant with a panoramic view of the Maspalomas dunes. A good choice for couples.

Gold by Marina €€ *Avenida Estados Unidos 15, tel: 928 948 555.* This cool adults-only hotel brightens gallery-white walls with playful Art Deco flourishes. An interior courtyard is a fun hangout when you're not lounging by one of two swimming pools or indulging in a soul-soothing spa treatment at the Gold Wellness Cottage.

Gran Canaria Princess €€€ *Avenida de Gran Canaria 18, tel: 928 768 132*, www. princess-hotels.com. This adults-only hotel, just a ten-minute walk from the beach, has a soothing wellness centre with Balinese daybeds and outdoor massage tables for alfresco treatments. Elsewhere, there are several swimming pools and sports facilities, while the basement restaurant is illuminated by glittering chandeliers.

Seaside Sandy Beach €€€ *Avenida Menceyes, tel: 928 724 000*, www.hotel-sandy-beach.com. Moorish influences pervade at *Seaside Sandy Beach*, from ornate wooden furniture in guest rooms to carved mirrors and earthy tiles in the lobby. Outside, an oval-shaped swimming pool is encircled by gently nodding palms and tropical plants. Both the beach and the centre are a short walk away.

Puerto de Mogán

Cordial Mogan Playa €€€ *Avenida de los Marrero, tel: 928 724 100*, www. cordialresortholidays.com. Stunning hotel designed in colonial style, with an esteemed restaurant and a swimming pool set in tropical gardens, all against a mountainous backdrop. Even the atrium is impressive, with wooden bridges straddling streams and waterfalls.

Radisson Blu Resort & Spa, Gran Canaria Mogan €€€ *Avenida de los Marrero 35, tel: 928 150 606.* Minimalistic decor runs throughout, and you'll notice a laidback atmosphere, too. For food and drink, there's the buffet-style *Larder Restaurant* plus an excellent Italian eatery and three fantastic bars. Elsewhere, you'll find a soothing spa, three heated swimming pools (including one seawater option), a sun-drenched outdoor terrace, fully equipped gym and yoga classes.

San Agustín

Paradisus Gran Canaria €€€€ *Calle Retama 3, tel: 928 774 090,* www.melia. com. A stunning all-inclusive resort in a prime spot alongside San Agustín Beach, where the elegant interior immerses you in luxury. There's a wide selection of rooms; pick of the bunch is a sea-view suite with a whirlpool on the balcony. The crop of global restaurants includes a buzzy adults-only beach club.

Amadores

Gloria Palace Amadores Thalasso & Hotel €€€ *Calle La Palma 2, tel: 928 128 510,* www.gloriapalaceth.com. This grand abode is built into the cliff overlooking the Atlantic, with a panoramic lift whisking guests down to the oceanfront promenade that leads to both Puerto Rico and Amadores beaches. The architecture is designed to resemble a cruise ship, with the ocean-view *Bar Salon* representing the bow. Elsewhere, you'll find two outdoor pools and a 1800-square-metre thalassotherapy centre with thirty treatment cabins.

Gloria Palace Royal Hotel & Spa €€€ *Playa Amadores, Calle Tamara 1, tel: 928 128 640,* www.gloriapalaceth.com. Poised on the cliffs above the picturesque Amadores Beach, this attractive hotel is connected to the waterfront promenade below by a glass-fronted lift. Built from local stone, it has been sensitively designed to blend in with the environment. Far-reaching ocean views steal the show here, best taken in from the gleaming infinity pool.

APARTMENTS, BUNGALOWS AND VILLAS

Gran Canaria has a wide variety of high-quality affordable accommodation in the tourist areas, including aparthotels, apartments, bungalows and villas. Check the following hotel groups for more details:

BE CORDIAL www.becordial.com
BULL HOTELS www.bullhotels.com
DUNAS HOTELS www.hotelesdunas.com
LABRANDA www.labranda.com
LIVVO HOTEL GROUP www.livvohotels.com
SERVATUR www.servatur.com

CASAS RURALES AND NATURE ESCAPES

In addition to the accommodation listed below, Gran Canaria Natural and Active offers a variety of rural and nature-based hotels and houses; check the website www.grancanarianaturalandactive.com for more information and to book.

Escuela Rural Casa de los Camellos €€ *Calle El Progreso 12, tel: 928 785 003,* www.hotelcasaloscamellos.com. An attractive *turismo rural* hotel, with twelve traditionally furnished rooms arranged around a shady courtyard. Run by HECANSA, the Canaries' official hospitality organization, *Casa de los Camellos* has an – unsurprisingly – good restaurant and bar and friendly, helpful staff. Packed lunches can be made if required.

Finca Las Longueras €€ *Valle de Agaete, tel: 928 898 145,* www.laslongueras. com. At the bottom of the main road between Agaete and Los Barrazales, this nineteenth-century red-brick mansion has been converted into a beautiful *casa rural*. There are nine carefully furnished en-suite rooms and junior suites with great views, a small swimming pool, and good Canarian food served in a tranquil setting.

Hotel Rural Las Calas €€€ *Calle El Arenal 36, San Mateo, tel: 655 647 498,* www.hotelrurallascalas.com. Just 3km (2 miles) outside Vega de San Mateo, this intimate hotel offers tranquillity and comfort. Set in lovely grounds, with a kitchen-garden that provides fresh vegetables for the restaurant, it has nine individually designed guest rooms. An excellent base for exploring Tejeda and Roque Nublo.

La Hacienda del Buen Suceso €€€ *Carretera Arucas–Bañaderos Km1, Arucas, tel: 928 622 390,* www.haciendabuensuceso.com. Set on a banana plantation just outside town, this lovely *hacienda* has eighteen rooms, each individually furnished with antiques and opening onto sofa-topped balconies. There is a pretty courtyard and garden, a small heated swimming pool, a steam room and whirlpool, a large barbecue area and a decent restaurant using lots of local, seasonal produce.

Occidental Roca Negra €€ *Avenida de Alfredo Kraus 42, Puerto de las Nieves, tel: 928 898 009,* www.barcelo.com. Built into the volcanic rock, this adults-only hotel is in a remote spot with panoramic views across the mountains down to the sea, and across to Tenerife. The 140 elegant rooms are spacious and feature either a balcony or terrace. Extensive facilities include a swimming pool, spa and rooftop restaurant.

Parador Hotel de Cruz de Tejeda €€€ *Cruz de Tejeda s/n, tel: 928 012 500,* www.parador.es. Located at one of the highest points on the island, *Parador Hotel de Cruz de Tejeda* makes the most of its prime perch with an outdoor terrace framing spectacular views. A clutch of wooden-beamed rooms has been beautifully refurbished, and the excellent restaurant serves authentic Canarian cuisine.

INDEX

THE **MINI** ROUGH GUIDE TO
GRAN CANARIA

Second Edition 2023

The Mini Rough Guide to Gran Canaria was produced in partnership with Turismo de Gran Canaria

Editor: Joanna Reeves
Author: Pam Barrett
Updater: Jackie Staddon
Cartography Update: Katie Bennett
Layout: Grzegorz Madejak
Head of DTP and Pre-Press: Rebeka Davies
Head of Pictures: Tom Smyth
Head of Publishing: Sarah Clark
Photography Credits: All images **Turismo de Gran Canaria** except: 141 Leading Hotels of the World; 4BR, 6T, 6B, 7T, 7B, 90, 102 Shutterstock
Cover Credits: The Dragon's Tail, Guayedra **Turismo de Gran Canaria**

Distribution
UK, Ireland and Europe: Apa Publications (UK) Ltd; sales@roughguides.com
United States and Canada: Ingram Publisher Services; ips@ingramcontent.com
Australia and New Zealand: Booktopia; retailer@booktopia.com.au
Worldwide: Apa Publications (UK) Ltd; sales@roughguides.com

Special Sales, Content Licensing and CoPublishing
Rough Guides can be purchased in bulk quantities at discounted prices. We can create special editions, personalised jackets and corporate imprints tailored to your needs. sales@roughguides.com; http://roughguides.com

Contact us
Every effort has been made to provide accurate information in this publication, but changes are inevitable. The publisher cannot be held responsible for any resulting loss, inconvenience or injury sustained by any traveller as a result of information or advice contained in the guide. We would appreciate it if readers would call our attention to any errors or outdated information, or if you feel we've left something out. Please send your comments with the subject line "Rough Guide Mini Gran Canaria Update" to mail@uk.roughguides.com.